It's not really a decision. It's a message from my body, which knows something I don't know. It makes me act, makes me get moving.

I'm too big for this egg, and when I move I break my shell.

I'm too big. I need to get out of this nest . . .

out of this hole . . .

head for the light, head downhill.

Where to?

To the sea.

What for?

To swim.

Why do that?

It's instinct, something inside that tells me what to do and makes me what I am.

I'm headed for something big,
    something bigger,
        the biggest thing in the world.
            I've got to get to the water.
                At last!
                    I'm headed . . .

KAREN ROMANO YOUNG

Across the Wide Ocean

The Why, How, and Where of Navigation for Humans and Animals at Sea

Greenwillow Books
An Imprint of HarperCollinsPublishers

Many thanks to: Paul Beach, U.S. Navy Submarine Squadron Support Unit • Karen Bjorndal, Archie Carr Center for Sea Turtle Research, University of Florida, Gainesville • Moira "Moe" Brown, Joanne Jarzobski, and Scott Landry, Provincetown Center for Coastal Studies • Craig Cary, Dave Barczak, and Tracey Bryant, University of Delaware • Craig Dickson, Shelley Dawicki, Susan Parks, Phil Richardson, Joanne Tromp, and Raul Martinez, Woods Hole Oceanographic Institution • Randy Kochevar, Monterey Bay Aquarium • Scott Kraus, New England Aquarium • Ken and Catherine Lohmann, University of North Carolina • Michael Moore and his family • Anna Moscrop and Rosemary McCaffery, International Fund for Animal Welfare • Sally Murphy, South Carolina Department of Natural Resources • John Allman, California Institute of Technology • Julia K. Baum and Ransom A. Myers, Dalhousie University • Sarah Bouchard, Otterbein College • Russell Byington, U.S. Department of Transportation Maritime Administration • Amy Holt Cline, University of New Hampshire • Tim Cole, National Marine Fisheries Service • Darlene Crist, Census of Marine Life • Sarah Dawsey, Cape Romain Wildlife Sanctuary • Annette deCharon, Bigelow Laboratory for Ocean Sciences • Peter Green, Central Fisheries Board, Ireland •Joan Hall and Victoria Kann, School of Visual Arts • Peter Keyes, Ned Moran, and Kimberly Shelley, Moran Towing Corporation • Deborah Kovacs • Chris McNally, St. George's School • Tom Morrisson, Sea Scouts • Mayra Pazos, NOAA Office of Oceanic and Atmospheric Research • Douglas Quine • Captain George Sandberg, U.S. Merchant Marine Academy • Astrid Schnetzer, University of California, San Diego • Leslie Smith, U.S. Navy • Jacob Vorhees • SSV *Geronimo* • SSV *Song of the Whale* • *Rosita* • *The Lucky Duck* •*Not By Bread Alone* •RV *Challenger* • Catherine Turecamo • RV *Atlantis* and DSV *Alvin* and their brave, true crews • Rebecca Davis and Sylvie LeFloch—yeah! • Mark, as always •

• • • • • • • •

Library of Congress Cataloging-in-Publication Data Young, Karen Romano. Across the wide ocean / by Karen Romano Young. p. cm. "Greenwillow Books."
ISBN-10: 0-06-009086-3 (trade bdg.) ISBN-13: 978-0-06-009086-9 (trade bdg.)
ISBN-10: 0-06-009087-1 (lib. bdg.) ISBN-13: 978-0-06-009087-6 (lib. bdg.)
1. Marine animals—Behavior—Juvenile literature. 2. Animal navigation—Juvenile literature. 3. Navigation—Juvenile literature. 4. Ocean—Juvenile literature.
I. Title. QL122.2.Y68 2006 623.89—dc22 2005046146

First Edition 10 9 8 7 6 5 4 3 2 1   Greenwillow Books

Table of Contents

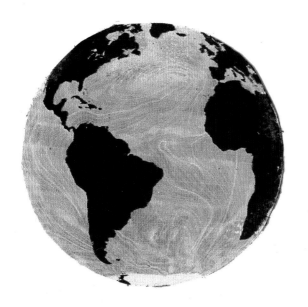

This map shows how fast water on the surface of the ocean is moving. Yellow stands for the fastest current; blue shows the slowest. It's a beautiful map, but what I like best is how the ocean and land look. Notice how the land is just black shadows, dropped out as though it was cut from the paper. In this map, the ocean is where it's happening.

*T*his is Emily. She was born in March, under the sign of Pisces, the fish. She loves to be in the water, loves to swim, loves to be wet. Emily would swim or take showers all day if she could. She doesn't know why. She just feels that she has to. It's her *instinct*.

When Emily was small, she loved to fall asleep in my lap in the beach chair, the waves playing cadences on her eardrums.

What do you do while someone sleeps in your lap for hours? Can't read. Can't eat. *Can* stare at the ocean and think how far it goes, how deep it is. *Can* watch what it does:

- Dolphins are out there, not far from shore, making a circle to herd fish together, catch and eat them.

- Pelicans skim the waves, filling their pouches with fish.

- Jellies wash up . . . scallop shells . . . . clam shells . . . a dead stingray.

- Fishing boats disappear over the horizon.

On a clear day, the horizon is about five miles away.

What? All I can see is five miles? But Spain is three thousand miles away. What's out there? What's *out* there?

"The people along the sand
All turn and look one way.
They turn their back on the land.
They look at the sea all day."
—Robert Frost, from
"Neither Out Far Nor In Deep"

Instinct is a feeling that you must do something. Looking for food is an instinct. Heading for the ocean is an instinct for hatchling sea turtles. And people? Do we have ocean-y instincts? Here's a thought: All life began in the oceans. About 70 percent of Earth's surface is now covered in water. Babies' bodies are about 70 percent water, too. (We lose water as we grow up.) This book is about how we find our way in the ocean—all of us—fish, people, other mammals, and other creatures.

I heard about a container (the box an eighteen-wheel truck hauls) that fell off a container ship during a storm. Its cargo was televisions that spilled out and floated all over the ocean until they washed up on beaches. What if they could tell their stories? What if you could turn them on and each one would show you where it had been?

The ocean is our unknown territory close to home. Although people have mapped 100 percent of the moon's surface, we have only seen less than 5 percent of the ocean floor. Every day we discover something new. New, alien-looking creatures, some with abilities hard for landlubbers to imagine. New ways of living. New ways of eating. New ways of traveling—and figuring out where they're going. It's extraordinary. If only we could turn on those televisions and tune in to places all over the ocean . . .

Well, it's covered with water, and the moon is not!

Did somebody say "TUNA?"

No tuna fish. Not yet.

We're here! Following the little fishes!

Not so easy to find, tuna. Elusive!

Big word.

Too soon for tuna. More about them later.

It means we get away fast.

7

The big picture looks something like this.

*T*here are so many fish and other creatures in the ocean that thousands have never been named or even seen. Down deep, on the bottom, tube worms and clams live rooted in one place. But most things in the ocean are on the move, going somewhere. Many stay in a small area. The ones in this book go a long way.

NORTH ATLANTIC OCEAN

A sailboat, the sloop *Rosita*, leaves the harbor at Sesuit, Massachusetts, and charts a course to Dublin, Ireland. The sailors keep their eyes peeled for the rare and mysterious North Atlantic right whale.

A loggerhead sea turtle hatchling north of Charleston, South Carolina, makes it to the surf, through the breaking waves, and to the ocean beyond.

*O*ff the coast of Georgia, a right whale and her newborn calf edge away from the birthing grounds and swim north. Hungry? This mama hasn't eaten for months.

8

*I*n the far north, a nuclear submarine emerges from beneath the polar ice cap in the Arctic Ocean and heads south between icy Greenland and green Iceland. Destination? Top secret!

A container ship threads the needle through the Strait of Gibraltar. Leaving the home port of Naples, Italy, behind, the captain sets a course west, for New York City.

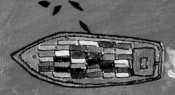

*W*hy are we earthlings—people and animals—such travelers? Where are we going?

*I*n the east Atlantic, a blue shark is on the trail of the elusive tuna . . . and he's not the only one.

And here the story begins . . .

9

Sea Turtle

Loggerhead sea turtle
(Caretta caretta)

Loggerheads hatch at roughly half this size (1.5–2 inches).

*I*t's a matter of life and death. Death to stay on the beach, easy pickings for predators like gulls or crabs. Life to make it to the ocean and out to sea. Some baby loggerheads can't find the water. Some get confused by lights. Some are eaten. But they *all* try.

How do they know where to go? How can they have a sense of direction when they've only just hatched? The answer comes in something the turtles have inside their bodies: their *genes.*

 ? No.

Genes are what make the turtle a turtle. They give its body directions on how to develop characteristics like sex and color, and instincts like hiding inside its shell and getting to the ocean quickly.

It's as if turtles are little robots, programmed to find the sea. Ken Lohmann, a biologist at the University of North Carolina, calls it genetic hardwiring.

Sarah Dawsey of Cape Romain National Wildlife Refuge in South Carolina makes sure loggerheads get the best start in life.

Sea turtles, he says, are hardwired to do three things in order to get from their nests to the open ocean where they will spend their lives.

1. USE THEIR EYES: Light attracts the hatchlings. Even on the darkest beach, the ocean reflects some light, making it brighter than the land and the sand dunes where the nests are dug.

2. USE THE WAVES: Once the light leads hatchlings to the ocean, why don't they get washed back in? At the shore, the waves come directly toward the beach. So diving into them leads turtles out to sea. Like surfers, little turtles point their heads straight into the waves and soon get beyond the breakers.

3. USE THEIR INNER COMPASS: As the water gets deeper, the waves go in all directions and stop showing the way, but turtles continue to swim straight out to sea. Ken Lohmann says that they use Earth's magnetic field to stay on course. More about the turtle compass soon.

Hatchlings sometimes turn toward lights on land. They wander in circles under streetlamps until seagulls pick them off, and are often smashed by cars. Scientist Blair Witherington identified what sort of light attracts turtles and helped Florida officials choose streetlamps that hatchlings will actually turn away from.

Loggerheads

- come from nests of 100 to 126 eggs that incubate for fifty to sixty days in holes about eighteen inches deep.
- lay 68,000 to 90,000 clutches of eggs a year from Texas to Virginia. Only about half of the eggs hatch.
- nest on the east coast of the U.S. and may travel all the way to the Mediterranean Sea.
- have related populations that nest in Australia, Oman, Japan, Brazil, South Africa, and the Yucatan Peninsula in Mexico.

11

*T*ry this: place your finger anywhere on these pages and hold it there. Now describe the spot where your finger landed. Use the markings on the page.

First, are you to the right or left of point zero? (You could also call this east or west, or positive or negative.) How far from zero are you? Next, how far above or below (north or south, or positive or negative) point zero are you?

Scientists who study how *all* earthlings find their way around say that the best way-finders use *true navigation*. That is, they use two pieces of information. One isn't enough. True navigation lets you find your destination when you're in an unfamiliar situation. To do this, you need to know:

which way + how far
direction + distance
x + y
intensity + inclination (more about these soon)
latitude + longitude

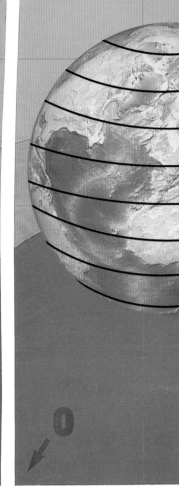

Y
North

0

West

South

• *On the globes above, the longitude lines are vertical (up and down). The latitude lines are horizontal (sideways). Draw a line all the way around a globe, and what do you get? A circle.*

• *On a globe, the y line is the prime meridian (the zero line for longitude). It passes through Greenwich, England, and through the north and south poles.*

• *On a globe, the x line is the equator (the zero line for latitude).*

Like any circle, longitude and latitude lines are divided into 360 degrees. And each degree is divided into sixty minutes. If you can figure out your longitude and latitude on the ground or on the ocean, you can find out where you are on your map. For people, longitude and latitude are keys to navigation. They unlock the secret of Where I Am.

• *The North Pole is ninety degrees north of any point on the equator. The South Pole is ninety degrees south of the equator.*

Longitude tells you how far east or west of the Y line (point zero) you are. Latitude tells you how far north and south of the X line (point zero) you are.

What if you, like animals, don't have a map? What helps you?

 Sight?   **Sound?** **Smell?**   **Touch?** **Taste?**  **Or another sense????**

Are animals true navigators? It's hard to tell. Some animals can find their way home even if they're moved many miles away. Scientists test this by "displacing" their subjects and watching to see if they can make it home. Homing pigeons and many other birds, alligators, and eastern red-spotted newts, as well as some dogs, cats, and people, can *home*. But are they true navigators?

There's no way of knowing for sure all the methods animals use. They could rely on the light of the moon, the sun, or the stars. Or the shape of the land, rivers, or coast. Landmarks. The tone and echo of sounds. Earth's magnetic pull. Temperature. Smell. Or something more.

People are the only earthlings who use maps. Humans have a particular part of the brain, the hippocampus, where maps and map knowledge are kept. People like taxi drivers, who need more maps "upstairs," have bigger hippocampus regions than other people.

Lost?

Grown-ups and babies. Turtle-wise, that's what we see along the east coast of the U.S. The babies hatch, they swim away, and they are not seen again in this area until they have twenty-inch shells, eight to twelve years later.

When Archie Carr began studying loggerheads in the 1940s, nobody knew where they spent their "lost" years. There was no way—yet—to tag or trail turtles that disappeared into the surf.

Carr gathered information from around the world that gave him clues to what the turtles were doing (surfing the Gulf Stream, a river of current that crosses the Atlantic) and where they went (across the wide ocean and back again). His theory wasn't proven until after he died in 1987.

1. Hatchlings swim out from shore to the Gulf Stream, a powerful ocean river of warm water . . .

2. . . . which carries them around the Sargasso Sea, where a sea of sargassum weed drifts on the surface, providing a kind of raft where turtles can float along, hidden. Their main meal along the way: jellyfish, other good drifters.

3. After about a year, turtles have drifted to the eastern Atlantic on their way to . . .

4. . . . the Azores. The bigger they get, the easier it is to swim where they want to go and not just get swept along in currents, eddies, whirlpools, and the big Gulf Stream.

5. Turtles spend eight to ten years in the eastern Atlantic, mostly at the surface. They turn west and follow the current back to the . . .

6. . . . Caribbean Sea, before going north to find food (conchs and crabs) along the southeast U.S. coast. Some bypass the Caribbean and go straight to the East Coast. The turtles are bottom dwellers now.

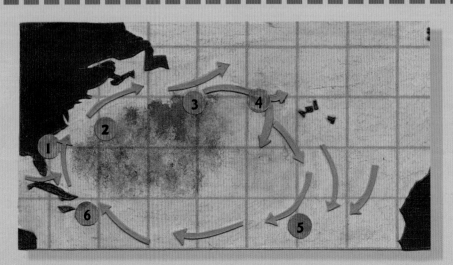

North
Atlantic
Drift

4

Now you know where turtles go. But you don't know how they know. (Read on, Sherlock.)

Round trip: Nine thousand miles

Do turtles have maps in their heads? Probably not. Animals don't have the mapping part of the brain—the hippocampus—that people have.

Bees do a dance, showing each other the design or shape of a trail to nectar.

Ants make a trail of scent called **pheromones** to lead the way to food.

Salmon use smell, too. They remember the smell of the river where they hatched from eggs. Years later, when it's time for them to spawn (fertilize and lay eggs), they travel from far out in the ocean to the exact river where they came from.

Sharks, of course, follow their big noses to fresh blood. More on sharks to come. On land, using your sniffer isn't unusual. Dogs do. Cats, too. Even people have been known to track down food by smell. (Try popping popcorn without attracting a crowd.)

When it comes to long-distance migrations, the sun may play a part. It takes a year for Earth to circle the sun, and at each point in the orbit the sun falls at a slightly different angle. Birds that fly to different places seasonally may take off instinctively when the sunlight falls at a specific angle.

Birds, like people and other animals, use *visual cues*—things they see—as guidelines. Coastlines, roadways, and mountain ranges can keep birds moving in the right direction.

But many creatures have a little something extra.

Loggerheads do. So may reptiles, amphibians, birds, honeybees, and possibly others. They use their eyes to receive light, their ears to receive sound, their noses to receive odors, their tongues to receive tastes, and their skin to receive information through touch.

Loggerheads also have receptors that give them information about the magnetic field around the Earth. As they travel, they use this special sense to decide *which way to go.*

In the lab, birds that usually fly south in November lined up on the south side of their cages when scientists Kenneth and Mary Able copied the angle of November light. The experiment worked even with young sparrows that had never migrated before.

Magnetic Force

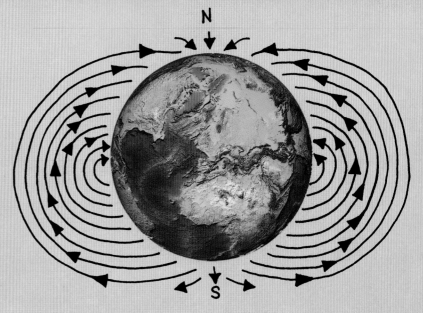

Planet Earth is an enormous magnet. The magnetic force flows through the center of the Earth, going in at the North Pole, out from the South Pole. Then it flows around the planet on the outside and back in at the North Pole.

This force is called Earth's *magnetic field.* Look at how the lines and arrows of the field appear on the picture of the Earth. It's like this all the way around the globe, with the field flowing parallel to the Earth at the equator and flowing in or out at steeper angles the closer you get to the poles.

North Pole   **South Pole**

This angle of inclination is also called *dip.* The force is stronger in some places than others, and the amount of strength is called *intensity*.

Each point on Earth has its own specific magnetic levels. If you know the dip and intensity of the magnetic field where you are—on land or at sea—you can figure out where you are on Earth.

Flip back to the turtle turning point on page 15. This place, west of the Azores, is where the Gulf Stream splits. Turtles need to take the south fork, toward Africa and warmth. Turtles that turn north could wind up frozen, washing up cold-stunned or dead on beaches in England or Norway.

Ken and Catherine Lohmann, marine biologists at the University of North Carolina, knew that most turtles turned. But *why?* The only way to find out was to copy what the magnetic field was like at the turning point and see what made the turtles turn.

Researchers say that turtles learn the intensity and inclination of the magnetic field at their native beaches and that this gives them a starting point for an inner map of the ocean.

THE TURNING   TURTLE EXPERIMENT

1. The Lohmanns got permission to "borrow" hatchlings. Loggerheads are threatened, which means they could become extinct if not protected.

2. They built a swimming tank in their laboratory. Around the tank, a big system of electric coils was made from strands of wire. When hooked up to a computer, the coils could make the magnetic field in the pool of water just like it is at the turning point near the Azores.

3. They made bathing suits for the tiny turtles.

    ?

No . . .

Ken Lohmann says, "We put each turtle into a little nylon-Lycra harness. It's basically just a little bathing suit for turtles. We attach a string to the harness. We can then tether the

turtle in a pool of water so the turtle swims, but it doesn't notice it isn't going anywhere."

4. As the turtles swam, the Lohmanns changed the magnetic inclination and intensity. And when the magnetic conditions matched those at the turning point, the turtles turned.

Q How does it work?

A Nobody's sure what makes the Earth magnetic in the first place. Most likely the core of molten (hot to the melting point) iron and nickel gets the magnetic flow flowing. The part of an animal that receives information about the magnetic field has iron in it. This part is called the *magnetoreceptor*.

Q Does this mean a turtle pictures the North Atlantic the way a person can?

A Probably not. An adult turtle's brain is only about the size of an adult human thumb, and the turtle doesn't have a hippocampus (the map storage part).

Turtle navigation might work more like tuning a radio. When the turtles are on the right track, all seems clear. When they go off course, they sense something like static.

Q Can people do it?

A ☑ squid   ☑ oysters   ☑ salamanders
☑ clams   ☑ octopi   ☑ honeybees
☑ dolphins   ☑ birds
☑ slugs   ☑ mice

Scientists have studied some species of each.

□ humans

Humans may have magnetoreceptors. But we don't have a reason to use them, so they haven't developed. Humans just don't make long migrations relying on our senses. We name and number directions. We use tools and time. We map the stars and seas.

I thought she'd forgotten all about dip.

Not to mention intensity!

time for tuna?

No, but let's get back to the ocean.

17

People have created tools and instruments and methods for detecting all the information that animals can sense naturally.

The Vikings may have set crows free so they could watch the direction the crows flew to reach land.

The Chinese had invented the compass by 100 A.D., but didn't use it for

navigation. It was a tool for *feng shui,* the art of arranging a house in the best way. Italian navigator Flavio Gioia claimed he invented the compass; he didn't. The European record of the compass includes a note about it in 1187, in the writings of an English monk. Gioia claimed to have invented the compass around 1300: too late!

compass

sextant

It took several hundred years before sailors around the world knew about the compass. Columbus used one to sail west to the Americas. Columbus's compass kept him heading west, but he had no way to figure out how far west he had sailed.

marine chronometer

The compass shows which way is north. Its magnet lines up with Earth's magnetic field and points toward magnetic north.

Navigators of Columbus's time knew how to use a sextant to find their latitude. The sextant shows the angle of the sun, which tells sailors how far they are from the poles or equator—their latitude. People can use a sextant with certain stars, too. More about this later.

To find longitude—the east-west position—you need the time at where you are *and* somewhere else on Earth. So you need a clock that can keep time on a rocking, rolling ship. The *marine chronometer,* invented in the 1700s, helps tell longitude. It keeps the time at Greenwich, England, which is on the prime meridian—the "equator" of longitude. Sailors use the sun's position to find the time where they are at sea. By comparing their time with Greenwich time on the chronometer, they can figure out their longitude—how far east or west of the prime meridian they are.

GPS—the Global Positioning System—does the work of all of these. A system of satellites communicates with your GPS receiver to give your longitude and latitude, your position on the globe.

A magnetic map? Yes.

This map shows a part of Earth's magnetic field. By 1707, when this map was drawn, people had been using compasses to navigate for hundreds of years.

"Before the compass, night and fog and clouds promised equal terror, for a navigator had no reliable directions but the sun and stars on the featureless surface of the awesome sea."—Jan Adkins, *The Craft of Sail*

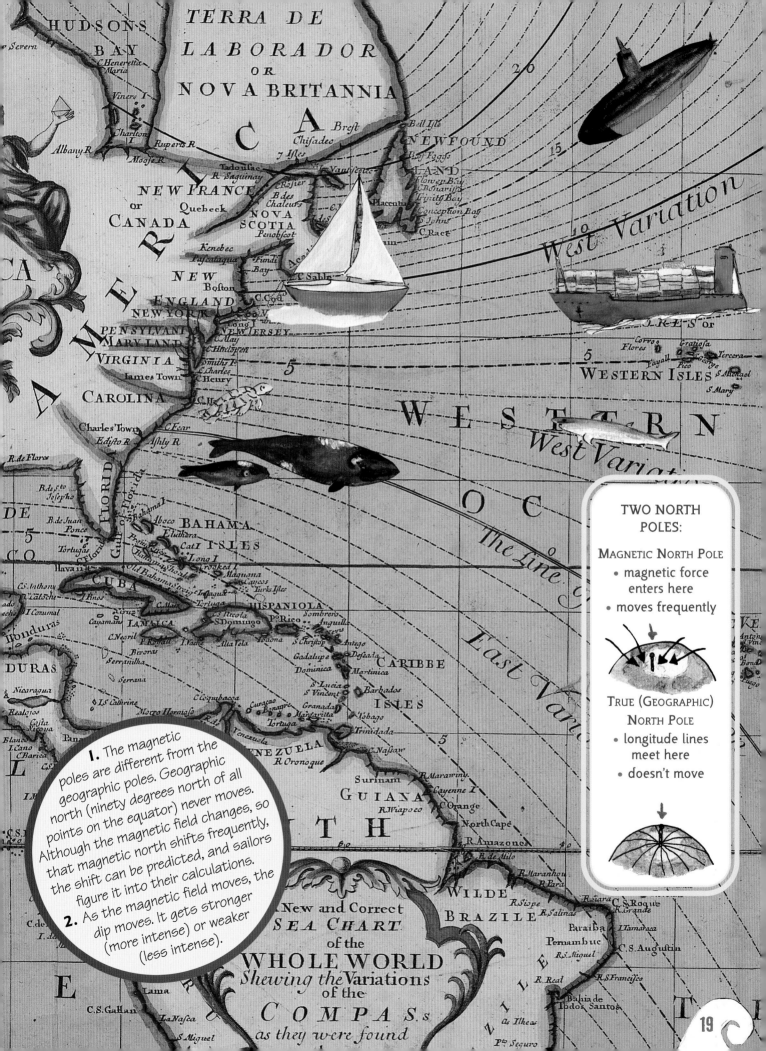

TERRA DE
LABORADOR
OR
NOVA BRITANNIA

HUDSONS
BAY

NEW FRANCE
or Quebeck
CANADA

NOVA
SCOTIA

NEW
ENGLAND
NEW YORK
PENSYLVANI
MARYLAND
VIRGINIA
CAROLINA

West Variation

NEWFOUND
LAND

WESTERN ISLES

W E S T E R N
West Variation

O C

The Line

BAHAMA
ISLES

CUBA

JAMAICA

HISPANIOLA

CARIBBE
ISLES

East Var

VENEZUELA

GUIANA

WILDE
BRAZILE

TWO NORTH POLES:

Magnetic North Pole
- magnetic force enters here
- moves frequently

True (Geographic) North Pole
- longitude lines meet here
- doesn't move

1. The magnetic poles are different from the geographic poles. Geographic north (ninety degrees north of all points on the equator) never moves. Although the magnetic field changes, that magnetic north shifts frequently, the shift can be predicted, and sailors figure it into their calculations.

2. As the magnetic field moves, the dip moves. It gets stronger (more intense) or weaker (less intense).

New and Correct
SEA CHART
of the
WHOLE WORLD
Shewing the Variations
of the
COMPASs
as they were found

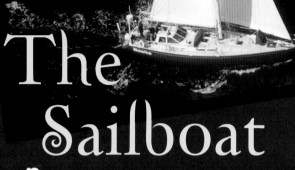

The Sailboat

Rosita is a fifty-five-foot sailboat that set out from Sesuit, Massachusetts.

Where to?

Dublin, Ireland, and back again, following the North Atlantic gyre (a river of current that circles the ocean).

What for?

A fourteen-month search for northern right whales.

Why do that?

Were the whales missing? Yes, you could say so. Woods Hole Oceanographic Institution biologist Michael Moore and the other scientists on *Rosita* knew that there were less than 350 right whales in the North Atlantic. They knew where some right whales were, most of the time: off Cape Cod in spring, off New Brunswick in summer, off the Georgia/Florida border in winter. . . .

The *Rosita* crew wondered where else the whales went, and had ideas about where to look for them. Michael had records of right whale hunts from many years ago. Those places in the ocean might still be whale habitat.

Way to go!

- Turtles don't give one another directions.
- Whales might communicate about their routes, or show their calves the way to go.
- People make maps of land and charts of the sea to show one another the way. People go to school to learn how to navigate.

Magnet School?

We School

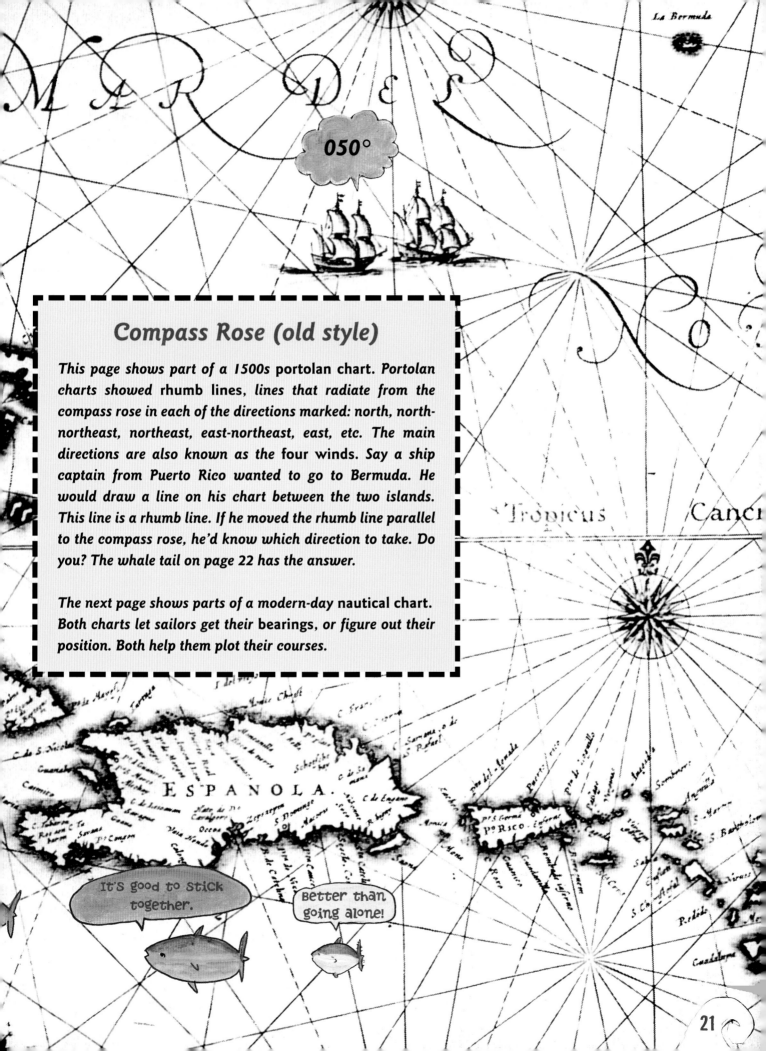

050°

Compass Rose (old style)

This page shows part of a 1500s portolan chart. Portolan charts showed rhumb lines, lines that radiate from the compass rose in each of the directions marked: north, north-northeast, northeast, east-northeast, east, etc. The main directions are also known as the four winds. Say a ship captain from Puerto Rico wanted to go to Bermuda. He would draw a line on his chart between the two islands. This line is a rhumb line. If he moved the rhumb line parallel to the compass rose, he'd know which direction to take. Do you? The whale tail on page 22 has the answer.

The next page shows parts of a modern-day nautical chart. Both charts let sailors get their bearings, or figure out their position. Both help them plot their courses.

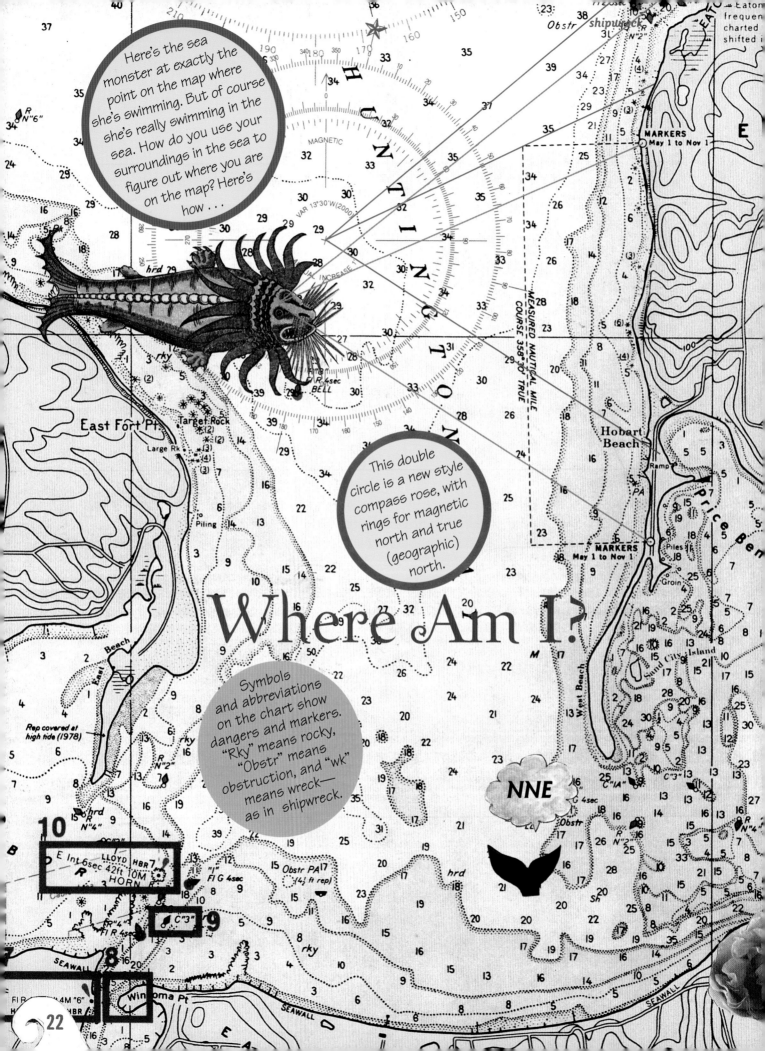

Here's the sea monster at exactly the point on the map where she's swimming. But of course she's really swimming in the sea. How do you use your surroundings in the sea to figure out where you are on the map? Here's how . . .

This double circle is a new style compass rose, with rings for magnetic north and true (geographic) north.

Where Am I?

Symbols and abbreviations on the chart show dangers and markers. "Rky" means rocky, "Obstr" means obstruction, and "wk" means wreck—as in shipwreck.

NNE

22

Compass Rose (new style)

*T*he old compass rose showed sixteen *directions*. Some larger roses showed thirty-two. On a new-style compass rose, the circle is divided into 360 *degrees*. Using numbers rather than direction names is more precise.

But why are there two circles? Remember the two North Poles—true (geographic) north and magnetic north? The outer ring lines up with true north. The inner ring lines up with magnetic north. Since your compass points to magnetic north, the magnetic ring is the one to use in most cases.

*S*hipwrecks aren't all bad . . . for fish. Shipwrecks make a shelter for sea animals. If you're a sea monster, they might seem like a seafood café, a good place to grab a quick bite. But how might the sea monster find the shipwreck? Real sea monsters don't have navigation devices. (But sea monsters aren't real.) This one demonstrates how to get your bearings and figure out what direction to take.

A sailor finds his position at the intersection of invisible streets, or lines of position

1. The sea monster surfaces and sights a lighthouse on the shore. She pulls out her trusty compass and takes a bearing. *The compass shows that the lighthouse is at an angle of 065°.*

2. The sea monster has visited other shipwrecks, and she has a nautical chart of her area. How fortunate!

There's a compass rose on the chart. She finds the 065° marking, but it's on the wrong part of the chart. So she uses parallel rulers to draw a line at the right angle. She places one ruler across the compass rose along the 065° mark. She uses the second ruler to draw a line to the lighthouse. She knows her position is somewhere on that line. But where is she on that line?

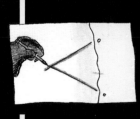

3. There's a smokestack on the chart . . . and she sights it! She uses it to draw another line, at 122°. This line and the line to the lighthouse are called lines of position. Her position is the place on the map where these two lines intersect. It's like telling somebody that your house is at the corner of State and Main.

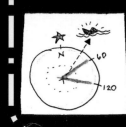

4. Now that she knows where she is, she can figure out what direction to take to find something else that's on the chart—the shipwreck. It's as if she's at the center of the compass rose. Remember to use the magnetic (inner) ring on the rose. Which direction—in degrees!—should she take to reach the shipwreck? The ship on page 21 has the answer.

Around the Ocean

The *Rosita* crew watched for whales . . . for container ships, fishing boats, and other traffic as they crossed the Boston shipping lanes . . . and kept track of wildlife twenty-four hours a day.

Michael Moore researched logbooks kept on whaling boats to find out where right whales were caught in the 1800s. Whalers hunted in the right whales' feeding areas, cold-water regions of Long Island, the Gulf of Maine, Newfoundland, Labrador, Greenland, Iceland, Spitsbergen (Norway), the Faroe Islands, Scotland, Ireland, and the Bay of Biscay. They also hunted in breeding areas, warm-water regions of the Azores, the Canaries, the Cape Verdes, Cintra Bay on the coast of Western Sahara, northern Florida, Georgia, and Bermuda.

Michael Moore knew about one whale, Metompkin, that didn't follow the path most other known right whales took. How does Michael know? Metompkin was tagged with a transmitter that sent information about her whereabouts to a satellite for several months, until the tag fell off mid-ocean. After losing her tag, Metompkin might have continued across the Atlantic to an area near the Azores.

Rosita's route will take her in a clockwise circle around the North Atlantic. Roughly speaking, she'll follow the North Atlantic gyre, the river of warm water the whales might follow, too (in bright green on the map below). She'll stop in Ireland, then turn south and sail for the Azores. She'll go south as far as Cintra Bay, hoping to find right whales along Metompkin's route or their old haunts. Then it's west and home with the northern equatorial current. (More on currents later.)

"We are looking for a few remaining right whale needles in the North Atlantic haystack."
—Michael Moore

Rosita's crew included Michael Moore, his wife Hannah, and his sons Oliver, Sam, Chris, and Tom.

* 05 11 00   42°03'N 45°03'W
STARTING A GREAT CIRCLE ROUTE TO IRELAND VIA A POSSIBLE RIGHT WHALE SPOT AT 49°N 22 W... LIFE IS GOOD. STILL LOOKING CLOSELY FOR ICEBERGS.   M.M.

GREENLAND
ICELAND
NEWFOUNDLAND
SCOTLAND
IRELAND
AZORES
LONG ISLAND
CAPE VERDE
CANARY ISLANDS
BERMUDA

North Atlantic right whale

Straight across the ocean?

The fastest way is to go straight, isn't it? Not on a round planet. To make a flat map of a round planet, you either lose correct direction (angle of travel) or correct distance. Different mapping methods are called *projections.* A Mercator projection shows distances properly, but not direction. A gnomonic projection shows direction correctly, but not distance. Just following a rhumb line (or heading continually in one direction) is longer than a great circle route. That's because when you follow straight lines, you have to keep turning to change your route. If Earth were a cube, a straight line would be *Rosita's* best bet. But on a sphere, swerve for the curve.

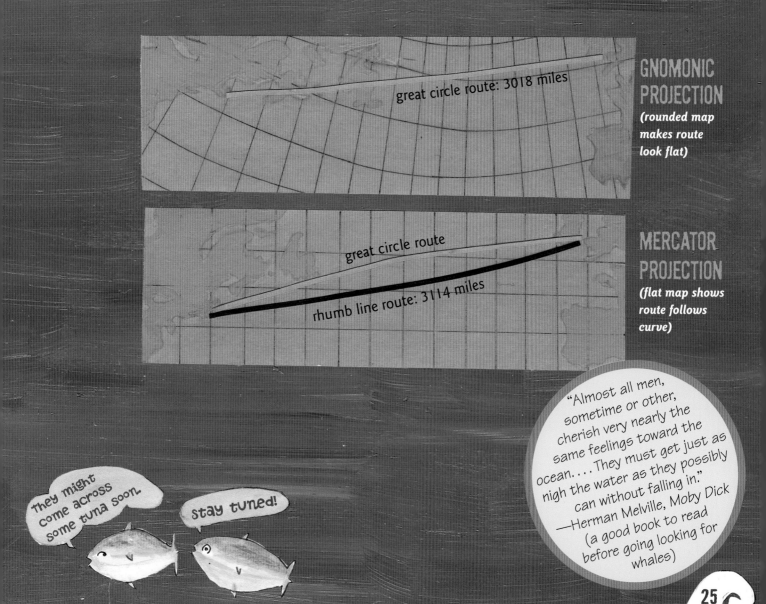

great circle route: 3018 miles

GNOMONIC PROJECTION
(rounded map makes route look flat)

great circle route

rhumb line route: 3114 miles

MERCATOR PROJECTION
(flat map shows route follows curve)

They might come across some tuna soon.

stay tuned!

"Almost all men, sometime or other, cherish very nearly the same feelings toward the ocean.... They must get just as nigh the water as they possibly can without falling in."
—Herman Melville, Moby Dick (a good book to read before going looking for whales)

At sea, finding your way without getting lost is all about time and all about space. To find your latitude, you use things in space: celestial bodies—the sun, moon, and stars. To find your longitude, you use time.

Sailors go to school to learn how to take a fix with a sextant.

Celestial Navigation

On a clear night, you can use the North Star,

Polaris, as a compass. In daytime, if you can see the sun, you can use a watch with hands as a compass. Point the hour hand at the sun. North is halfway between the sun and twelve.

Finding Latitude at Sea

How do you find the global position of a star? With a book called the *Nautical Almanac* and a simple shape: the triangle. Here's how a triangle can be used to help a sailor find his latitude.

A triangle has three angles and three legs. The angles of a triangle always add up to 180°.

Low-Tech Method

Over time, people have taken note of the global positions of fifty-seven stars—called the *navigational stars*—24/7, 365 days a year (366 in leap year). These numbers are found in the *Nautical Almanac* every ship carries.

1. Identify a star. Use a star chart, until you know your stars by heart.

2. Sight the star with your sextant to find its

angle above the horizon (you can use the moon, sun, and other planets, too). Note what time it is. Now you have the first angle of the triangle.

3. Find the star on the chart in the *Nautical Almanac*. It gives the *azimuth*, the global position of each navigational star for various times, as if a straight line were drawn from the star into the center of the earth. The angle the straight line forms as it connects with Earth is always a perfect right angle, ninety degrees.

Remember, all three angles add up to 180°. Now that you have two angles, you can subtract them from 180 to find the third. Next you plug your numbers into a formula. The *Nautical*

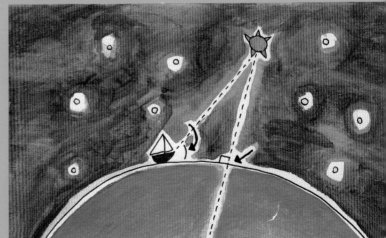

44° W

> "Even the moon, smiling wryly down on our efforts, can provide a useful signpost."
> —Tom Cunliffe, *Celestial Navigation*

Almanac will help you calculate position so that you can find your latitude on the map. This process is called taking a fix on a star. Sailors go to school to learn the fine points of this process and become experts at it.

High-Tech Method

More and more sailors rely on the data provided by the Global Positioning System (GPS). You can use a handheld GPS receiver or one that's part of a computer. But few sailors would go to sea without knowing the low-tech method.

Finding Longitude

For every fifteen degrees you travel east, local time moves forward one hour. Time moves back if you go west.

You can tell what time it is where you are by noting when the sun is at its high point at noon.

If you have the local time where you are on the ocean and the local time somewhere (anywhere) else on Earth, you can figure out your longitude. Say it's noon where your boat is, and your clock set on New York time reads 10 A.M. That's two hours west of you, or thirty degrees more. Your handy globe tells you that New York's longitude is 74° west. So what's your longitude? The moon has the answer.

The key is to keep time somewhere else while at sea. Clocks in the time of Galileo, Newton, and Halley had pendulums that got messed up by the motion of the ocean. From 1730 to 1770, John Harrison invented a series of clocks (called marine chronometers) that *didn't*. These clocks kept the time at Greenwich, England.

Watching the Stars Rise

The famous navigators of the Caroline Islands in the western Pacific use the whole dome of the sky as their compass. The places in the dome where each star rises and sets are their direction points rather than degrees. As children, the islanders begin to learn the routes to each island, using the paths between the rising and setting points of the stars. Caroline Islanders find their way over thousands of miles of ocean without sextants, chronometers, a Nautical Almanac, or any other tools—besides the ones in their heads. They read the winds, waves, and currents, too. They learn how these things relate to the compass in terms of angles and distances—and they develop a mental map of the islands, reefs, and other "seamarks."

This is a sidereal compass (a star compass). The circle of the horizon is divided into thirty-two points where the stars rise and set.

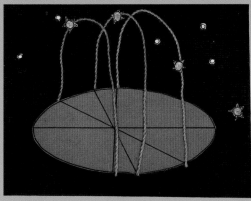

27

Navigation System

- **GPS.** A chart plotter (1) gives you your own GP (global position) and that of any waypoint (destination). It can give your range (distance) and bearing (course), too. A handheld GPS receiver (2) is an important piece of backup equipment.

- **LORAN** (not shown), or Long Range Aids to Navigation. LORAN stations onshore send out signals. Signals from two LORAN stations are combined to give a boat's position.

- **Radar.** Buoys, lighthouses, and other ships return radar signals a boat sends out. The boat's radar indicator (3) shows the distance and angle from these objects.

- **Compasses** show wind angle (4a) and direction of boat (4b). Direction is also displayed on a digital readout (5).

- **Speed over ground in knots** (6) shows speed of boat.

- **Trip log in nautical miles** (7) shows how far you've gone.

- **Dividers** (8) are used to find distance.

- **Nautical Almanac** (9) helps find positions, tides, stars, etc.

- **Chart** (10) is used to find position and plot course.

- **VHF,** or very high frequency, radio (11) lets you talk to other ships and people onshore, including the Coast Guard, at ranges of up to fifty miles. Handheld VHF (12) has a shorter range. VHF radios must be kept tuned to Channel Sixteen when you're not transmitting. That's the channel for sending distress signals. This way all ships are always listening, just in case someone needs help.

- **Single sideband radio,** or SSR (13), is on hand for longer distances. Sometimes you can get a clear SSR signal from ten thousand miles away!

- **A weather fax** (not shown) provides faxes of weather maps, sea surface temperature maps, wave height predictions, and other news about conditions.

This is my daughter Bethany in the bow of *Not By Bread Alone,* the sloop her Sea Scouts group sails. Bethany needs to be on the water. She thinks people's need for the ocean has something to do with the time before we were born, when we floated inside our mothers. Bethany is never more serene than when she's on a boat—at the tiller, studying the *Nautical Almanac,* or just waiting for the wind to pick up. Here, she's reading *Dove,* Robin Lee Graham's book about his sail around the world.

A *chart plotter* helps you track and plan your course. The screen shows the boat's position in relation to its destination and gives the course to follow.

Can't a *computer* help you navigate? Sure. Navigational computers are useful even to small sailboats. For example, computers can store all the information about stars, tides, magnetic variations, and more contained in the big, heavy *Nautical Almanac* and in rolls and rolls of charts. They can factor in GPS data, weather forecasts, wave height, temperature, and more. But . . . *you never can tell what might happen at sea.*

Michael Moore says, "I had tables and a good sextant. I don't think I took it out of the box once. The test of 'If we lay such-and-such a course, where will we be by dawn? . . . by next week?' is so much easier with a mouse than a pencil and a stack of paper charts."

That was true in the middle of the ocean, but "as we closed on specific hazards we tended to ignore the computer and the GPS, and resort to seat-of-the-pants eyeball coasting, as we have all done forever."

Moore goes on, "In reality our coastal piloting was done by my wife, Hannah, behind the wheel with a paper chart in hand, while I watched the computer screens below. We compared and contrasted our idea of the best line to follow. It seemed to work. The only time we ran aground was at the customs dock in Trinidad. Stay to the west end!"

WHAT IF your boat sinks?

An emergency raft with a sail and supplies for sixty days is what you need, says George Sigler. He made a study of survival at sea. If you can sail, you can survive, Sigler says. No place in the ocean is farther than two thousand miles—a sixty-day sail—from land.

> "The sextant is the key to it all. With this instrument, I measure the altitude above the horizon of the sun, moon or stars, then mark the time to the second on my chronometer. After that it's simply a matter of looking up the nautical tables, making additions and subtractions which wouldn't strain an average ten-year-old, and pinpointing my exact position on the charts. That's the theory. In practice mistakes can be made."
> —Robin Lee Graham, *Dove*

WHAT IF a great white shark chases your raft's fishing line?

> Robin Lee Graham sailed around the world by himself, starting from California at age sixteen and finishing when he was twenty-one.

That happened to Sigler on his trans–Pacific trip. His answer was to cut the fishing line . . . and the great white dove, and was gone.

WHAT IF you get hit by a ship?

John Oman's sailboat *Northwest Spirit* was hit by a Greek container ship, *Angelic Protector*. John used his VHF radio to contact the ship for help. "Bruised, shaken, we headed home," wrote John in his logbook. Although *Northwest Spirit's* mast was broken, the sailboat made it back to port.

WHAT IF a power failure knocks out your instruments?

Use navigation by *dead reckoning*. This method is like a giant using stepping stones to cross the water. The stepping stones are the points where you know your position. The strides in between require dead reckoning: you figure out where you are based on how far you've traveled since your last known position. If you lose track of your direction or how far you've come, you're lost.

Frigate birds and petrels stay at sea and can lead fishermen to fish. Seagulls sleep on land, so as night nears, you can follow them home.

> "I'm somewhere close to the island. I'm sure of that. But where is it? Pity there aren't any milestones in the sea."
> —Robin Lee Graham, *Dove*

container ship:
31°20'N, 22°50'W

turtle: 32°N, 50°W

shark: 40°N, 10°25'W

Meanwhile, back in the ocean . . .

Check the positions of Rosita and the other ocean travelers on the televisions. The numbers give latitude and longitude.

Remember, latitude tells you how far you are north or south of the equator, which is 0° latitude; 42°04'N means 42 degrees, 04 minutes north of the equator.

Longitude tells you how far you are east or west of the prime meridian, which is 0° longitude; 69°47'W means 69 degrees, 47 minutes west of the prime meridian.

How do you play *tag* with animals that can go where you can't? Satellites. If satellites can find the global position of boats, ships, and submarines, why not animals? No problem—as long as the animal has a tag with a GPS receiver or other equipment to communicate with the satellite. Satellite tagging (also called satellite telemetry) allows scientists to chase animals across the nautical miles and into the depths. The scientists don't have to move (once they've tagged the animals) to get a picture almost as good as a magic television.

Remember Metompkin, the right whale whose route Michael Moore's sailboat followed? Metompkin's journey was traced by WhaleNet's

You know, you can tune a tv. . . .

But you can't tune a fish!

unless it's tagged . . .

so tag me!

submarine:
58°10'N, 33°10'W

sailboat Rosita:
42°04'N, 69°47'W

right whale:
34°45'N, 75°20'W

Let's tune in and see what is happening.

Satellite Tagging Observation Program (STOP) and the New England Aquarium in Boston. Scientists also tune in to and study seals, porpoises, turtles, and other whales. VHF radio tags let researchers track animals swimming nearby. Satellite tags let them track animals that swim hundreds of miles away.

- Some tags only send signals when the animal is at the surface. But new pop-up tags store information while an animal is underwater, then pop up to the surface to transmit data about where the animal has been.
- Fishermen who used to catch and kill sharks now catch, tag, and release them. Each year the Center for Shark Research of Mote Marine Laboratory in Sarasota, Florida, sponsors the Gulf Coast Shark Census, a tournament for tagging sharks. Sharks may be caught with rod and reel or in gill nets, for tagging. Big sharks are netted, pulled close to the boat, and tagged using a pole.

- Tagging gives information on shark migration, age, growth, behavior, habitats, and death.

Scientist Sally Murphy tags adult female loggerheads to learn where they go when they are not laying nests of eggs. The turtles she studies lay their eggs on the beaches of Cape Romain National Wildlife Refuge in South Carolina. To tag a turtle, Sally's team places a box like this one around it.

"The turtle jams into a corner and stops," she says. The team uses paint scrapers and a wire brush to prepare the surface of the shell, then epoxy glue to attach the transmitter. Next the box is removed and the turtle returns to the sea. The data tell Sally that these mother turtles swim north and south, following the edge of the continental shelf, the point where the ocean floor drops off to the deep sea.

Right Whale

Good News

1998: 5 new calves seen	2002: 21 new calves seen
1999: 4 new calves seen	2003: 16 new calves seen
2000: 1 new calf seen	2004: 16 new calves seen
2001: 31 new calves seen	2005: 28 new calves seen

North Atlantic right whale
(Eubalaena glacialis)

*I*f you see, at the ocean's surface, a smooth, broad back the size of a school bus, and if the back has no fin, and if it is mostly black, with some patches of yellowish white skin, then you could be seeing one of the world's rarest animals: the North Atlantic right whale.

Right whales swim through waters rich with tiny krill and copepods. They take in huge mouthfuls of water and they use the baleen in their mouths as a screen or sieve. Water flows out through the openings in the baleen, and food stays in—up to two tons of it a day! But right whales don't eat every day. They eat most of their food off Massachusetts during the spring. In summer they travel to the Bay of Fundy, north of Maine, to mate. By winter they swim all the way to the border of Florida.

WHALE MIGRATION

Where to?

Mostly north and south from New Brunswick to Florida.

The purpose of Rosita's journey was to find new right whale habitats. Despite visiting many of the places right whales have been hunted or sighted in the past, Rosita's crew did not find a single right whale.

What for?

To eat, to mate, to give birth.

Why do that?

Different places have the ideal conditions for different activities.

Tracking whales on their migrations has helped scientists identify the most important right whale habitats. When they check the habitats, they only account for 75 percent of the right whales they know exist. Where do the others go?

Scientists from the Provincetown Center for Coastal Studies in Massachusetts help whale-watch boat captains in the Dolphin Fleet find whales for tourists to watch. PCCS naturalists identify individual whales. This information goes into a database at the New England Aquarium, which keeps track of the whales and their movements.

How do you find right whales?

"It's not an exact science," says Dr. Moira "Moe" Brown, Provincetown Center for Coastal Studies. "We go where we saw them last time. We find out where they were before. We go back to history. When we run out of that, we're just guessing."

Here are just a few North Atlantic right whales from the catalog: Shackleton, Van Halen, Churchill, Piper, Starry Night, Necklace. Some whales just have numbers.

For more than twenty-five years, the New England Aquarium has worked to put together a catalog of North Atlantic right whales. The whales can be identified by their head markings, called *callosities*, the bumps and lumpy patches on the whales' heads. At first the catalog consisted of photographs, but now a computer system helps whale sighters identify their whales.

Right whales follow this sequence when they dive. Dive sequences are one way whale watch guides identify different species of whale from a distance.

Right whales have two blowholes, so their spouts are V-shaped—one way to identify them.

callosities

In the good old days, right whales could be found all over the North Atlantic. Then came whalers, who called them right whales because they were the right ones to catch. Why?

1. They swam slowly and were easy to hunt.
2. When killed, they floated and could be towed ashore.
3. Their thick blubber yielded up to seventy barrels of oil for lamps and for lubricating machinery.

By 1900 right whales were hunted nearly to extinction in the North Atlantic. In 1935 hunting of right whales was banned in all the oceans. In the early 2000s, they are still very much in danger of becoming extinct.

Save that whale!

A Woods Hole Oceanographic Institution study shows that if conditions for right whales don't change dramatically, the species could become extinct in the next two hundred years.

Main problems for right whales:
- collisions with ships
- getting tangled in fishing equipment

Possible solutions:
- change shipping lanes
- improve methods of warning ships that whales are near
- use whale-friendly fishing gear

Other worries:
- pollution, including noise pollution (more on noise and whales later)
- gene variation: At this point, most right whales are kin to one another. It's not healthy for any species to breed too much with relatives.

Whale Tales

This map shows the route a tagged whale, Kingfisher, took from March 17 to April 4, 2004. Kingfisher, a one-year-old whale, was tagged after being spotted off the Florida coast. He was entangled in fishing line. Rough seas and storms kept disentanglement teams from helping him. Farther north, off the coast of Cape May, New Jersey, a fishing boat ran over the line attaching the tagging buoy to the whale, severing it. Would Kingfisher be found again? In January 2005, Kingfisher was sighted off the Georgia coast, still entangled but doing well. . . .

Canada

United States

Scott Landry of the PCCS used photographs and reports from the observers to draw the lines entangling Kingfisher. Whale rescuers used this drawing to make a plan for disentangling the whale. Although entanglements do kill whales (and other animals), Kingfisher survived.

Charles "Stormy" Mayo of the Provincetown Center for Coastal Studies cuts fishing line from the tail of a whale.

One whale's story

2001: Right whale #3120 was first seen as a calf, with his mother, in Cape Cod Bay.

Feb. 2002: #3120 was seen with his mother off Florida.

Apr. 7, 2002: A whale watch boat found #3120 badly entangled in lines off Cape Fear, NC.

May 24, 2002: #3120 was seen feeding with other whales, Great South Channel, MA.

July 25, 2002: Whale watchers see #3120 in the Bay of Fundy.

Aug. 25, 2002: Right whale researchers from Maine attached a satellite tag to the lines to help them keep track of his whereabouts, in hope of cutting off lines in the future.

Aug. 26, 2002: Some lines removed. #3120 kept making long dives to get away from the researchers. The tag came off with the lines, so researchers lost track of the whale.

Feb. 20, 2003: #3120 was seen off Jacksonville Beach, Florida. He seemed more healthy.

June 17, 2003: #3120 was sighted east of Massachusetts by aerial survey team. The whale was found feeding. He appeared to be in relatively good condition, despite continued entanglement.

There are fewer than 350 North Atlantic right whales left. Some die of natural causes, but many are hit by ships. Why?
- The whales' feeding, breeding, and calving areas are close to shore.
- Right whales move slowly, often too slowly to avoid ships, and even more slowly if they have calves with them.

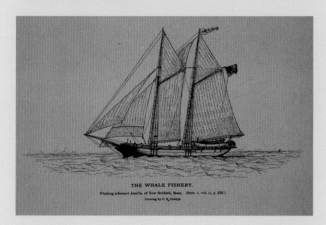

THE WHALE FISHERY.
Whaling schooner Amelia, of New Bedford, Mass. (Sect. v, vol. ii, p. 232.)
Drawing by C. S. Raleigh.

- It's hard for whales to be spotted by ships in time to avoid them. Just the flat portion of the back of a right whale shows above water.

Air surveyors report on whale sightings, so ships can avoid those areas. On the planes are a pilot, two observers, and someone to take notes and record data such as global position. The planes fly in grid patterns just 750 feet above the water.

Moe Brown led the effort to change shipping lanes in the Bay of Fundy so that ships headed for St. John, New Brunswick, would travel farther from whale grounds in the bay.

The Right Whale Sighting Advisory System (SAS) gets whale sighting reports from all over. It faxes and radios whale positions to everyone in the area as part of weather reports, traffic control directions, and Coast Guard news. Who sends sighting info?
- fishermen
- whale watch boats
- Coast Guard
- people onshore
- ferryboats
- the National Marine Fisheries Service
- scientists
- conservationists (people working to help wildlife)
- shippers
- air surveyors

Here are the results from one late December/early January week of Early Warning System flights off Jacksonville Beach, Florida.

2 Kemp's ridley sea turtles

444 bottlenose dolphins

136 loggerhead sea turtles

7 leatherback sea turtles

30 cownose rays

15 mola mola (ocean sunfish)

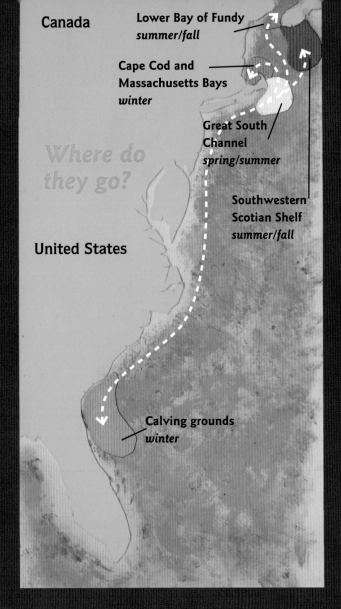

Canada

Lower Bay of Fundy
summer/fall

Cape Cod and
Massachusetts Bays
winter

Great South
Channel
spring/summer

Southwestern
Scotian Shelf
summer/fall

*Where do
they go?*

United States

Calving grounds
winter

- use Earth's magnetic field
- get information from the ocean currents
- *echolocate*, using sound to figure out where they are
- learn the route from following their mothers

Check that last idea again. Doesn't seem that odd, does it? Don't most of us learn things by following our parents around? Yes, but . . .

Learning a route by imitating another individual is a sign of a different level of intelligence than, say, a sea turtle has. Whales are *cetaceans*, the same family as dolphins. Many scientists believe cetaceans are smarter, more able to make certain kinds of decisions, and more able to learn things than your average sea dweller.

*T*he western North Atlantic right whales migrate up and down the coast of the U.S. and Canada. In winter, pregnant female right whales give birth off the coast of Georgia and Florida. At the end of February, males, and females that aren't mothers, feed east of Massachusetts at Stellwagen Bank on Cape Cod Bay. They are joined by mothers and calves in spring.

How do right whales know where they are going?

Scientists are trying to find out whether whales:
- use the stars
- recognize their route by detecting changes in the water's temperature, salinity (saltiness), or taste

such as a tuna?   pretty average.   speak for yourself!

Are whales who seem to travel on their own actually staying in touch with others hundreds of miles away?

Humans can't hear everything that dolphins and whales can. People used to think the undersea world was silent, before sound equipment was invented. Many dolphin and whale sounds fall outside the range of human hearing.

Echolocation is how dolphins know where they are and what's around them. Like bats, they let out high-pitched squeaks and chirps every so often. They use the echoes of the sounds to figure out how far they are from things.

Whales may use echolocation in a different way. Low-pitched (or low-frequency) deep whale sounds are called songs, because they follow patterns, as songs do. *Pods* (groups) of whales often sing the same songs. Could whales be using sound to communicate? Or could they be sending out their songs so far that they bounce off the sides of underwater mountains hundreds of miles away? For the whales, these mountains may act as mid-sea lighthouses, helping them figure out where they are in the ocean. (Some scientists ask, if baleen whales—such as right whales and sperm whales—use sound to find their way, why do they get hit by ships? Why don't they hear the ships?)

Boats use echolocation to find the depth of the water. A transducer called an echosounder mounted on a boat's hull sends a sound out toward the bottom and measures how long it takes to come back. The result shows an image of the seabed level.

Sailors always have a low-tech backup for any instrument. To check the accuracy of the echosounder, they drop a lead line (pronounced "led" line), marked with fathoms,

A ship aims multi-beam sonar onto a slice of ocean floor (left) and side-scan sonar from a tow (right).

meters, or feet, and with a weight tied to the end, which sinks to the bottom.

Sonar was invented in 1906 to help detect icebergs, but more ships began to use it in World War I, when submarines were lurking about. Just as echolocation naturally helps dolphins find fish, sonar mechanically helped ships find subs. At first sonar systems only "listened" for sounds. Eventually they became active, sending out their own signals as well.

Passive sonar systems let military ships listen without sending out a sound of their own. Scientists use passive sonar to avoid scaring the fish. Databases in the system match a sound profile with those of different kinds of ships or animals.

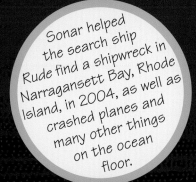

Sonar helped the search ship *Rude* find a shipwreck in Narragansett Bay, Rhode Island, in 2004, as well as crashed planes and many other things on the ocean floor.

Sonar stands for "sound navigation ranging." It's a system for detecting objects in the water.

Underwater Ears

The hydrophones many researchers use were once used by the military to listen for submarines.

- Some hydrophones are on the ocean floor.
- Some are towed underwater by ships.

Today people create so much underwater noise—drilling for oil, sending out sonar sounds, traveling in ships and subs—that scientists worry about the effects on whales, fish, and other sea creatures. Some even think that human sounds might confuse the navigational abilities of certain whales and dolphins. Sound might cause pods of whales to beach themselves. Nobody is sure, though, and the mystery of why whales beach themselves remains unsolved.

The U.S. Navy wants to use extra-low-frequency active sonar to look for foreign submarines that might threaten national security. In 2002 in the Canary Islands, after the navies of several different countries tested this powerful sonar, ten beaked whales beached themselves and died. Zoologists said the whales showed signs of "the bends"—a nickname for decompression sickness, which happens to scuba divers who come up too fast after a dive to deep water. Other whale beachings and deaths may have been caused by sonar in the waters where whales were swimming. The sound of this new sonar can reach levels as loud as a space shuttle taking off and can carry hundreds of miles. The U.S. Navy is working with scientists to try to understand the effect of sonar on whales, and says that new sonar methods might save whales by helping ships locate them underwater. Many countries have limited their use of sonar, and the U.S. may, too.

Sounds

About two-thirds of North Atlantic right whales spend May in the Great South Channel near Cape Cod, then swim north to the Bay of Fundy, off New Brunswick, in summer. Where does the other third go? Is it that easy to lose track of more than a hundred whales? It sure isn't easy to find them. . . .

Every minute of *Rosita's* voyage, the crew kept watching and listening for right whales. They kept track of all the different sounds and species they came across, for example:

"Dolphins."

"Pilot whales."

"Ship noise."

"Nuffink."

On page 39, a map of hydrophones in the east Atlantic shows spots where scientists listened for whales and other animals.

Acoustics is the science of sound. Underwater acoustics is being used to learn about—and protect—right whales. Ten years ago scientists weren't sure right whales made enough noise to be picked up on hydrophones, instruments that "hear" under the water. In 1997 the research vessel *Song of the Whale*, operated by the International Fund for Animal Welfare (IFAW), first towed hydrophones off the east coast of North America. They picked up enough right whale sounds to confirm that acoustics would be a good additional tool for detecting right whales, better than only watching for them from the surface or the air.

After that, *Song of the Whale* deployed pop-up buoys created at Cornell University's Bioacoustics Research Program. The pop-ups sit on the seafloor for four to six weeks, then pop up to the surface.

The map (below) shows places hydrophones were placed. Whale sounds "look" like this (right).

An island is a paradise after weeks at sea.

Other theories about why whales and dolphins beach themselves:
- the pod may follow a lost or sick member
- gently shelving beaches can mix up their navigation
- suicide
- illness
- undersea earthquake or volcanic eruption might distress them
- injury
- confusion
- disturbance in Earth's magnetic field caused by solar flares

The boat returns to pick them up and take them back to shore. While on the seafloor, the pop-ups gather recordings and other data, such as date, time, and temperature. The data on the pop-ups gave scientists Susan Parks and Darlene Ketten from Woods Hole Oceanographic Institution the information they needed to learn more about right whale sounds.

Along the coast, where right whales spend most of their time, passing ships create a lot of noise. Darlene and Susan have analyzed the ears of right whales in order to figure out what they can hear. "Right whales should be able to hear ships, based on the fact that their own vocalizations are in the same frequency range as much of a ship's noise," says Susan. "No one under-stands exactly why right whales get hit by ships. They might not be able to hear the ship, or they might hear it but not perceive it as a threat."

Now IFAW, Cornell, and others want to place hydrophones on permanent buoys in right whale habitat. The buoys will communicate via phone or satellite to let people know when a right whale is heard. Then the information can be added to the Right Whale Sighting Advisory System bulletins that inform ships that right whales are in the shipping lanes. Eventually, says IFAW's Anna Moscrop, these instruments could be placed in areas that *might be* right whale habitat. Right now, Anna says, priority goes to protecting whales in the areas we already know about.

Song of the Whale scientists deploy hydrophone buoys in the Great South Channel, hoping to pick up the sounds of right whales.

A buoy is ready to be deployed and inflates later so it can be retrieved.

In 2003 Scott Kraus of the New England Aquarium, Dr. Moira Brown, and other right whale experts sailed to old whaling grounds in the North Atlantic. Off Cape Farewell, the southern-most point of Greenland, they saw one right whale—a new one, never seen before. Could Cape Farewell be a habitat of the missing right whales?

What are they saying? What are they singing?

Here are the results of some research on baleen whale sounds.

- Male finback whales seem to call females to patches of food, where they mate.
- Blue whale and finback sounds can be heard beyond fifteen hundred nautical miles. That's about thirteen hundred statute (land) miles, the distance between New York and Miami.

- Sperm whales click about once per second as they dive into canyons in search of food. The echoes of their clicks reveal the location of the ocean floor, canyon walls, and prey. Their prey: giant squid!

What do right whales sound like?

- *ooooOOOO* (the "upcall" lasts about a second, with pitch getting higher)
- *OOOOoooo* (the "downcall" is the same length, with pitch getting lower)
- BANG (the "gunshot" sounds like whales are slapping the water, but the noise is actually produced inside the whales)
- EEEE! (like elephant sounds, made mostly by female whales)

Susan Parks provided this information and added: "Some tagging work on right whales

"Trying to detect whales by sight alone is like birding in a dense forest with your ears plugged."—Russ Charif, Cornell Bioacoustics Research Program

IFAW's Sarah Wong readies hydrophones on pop-up buoys that will be placed in the ocean off Massachusetts from the research vessel Song of the Whale.

" Acoustic detector buoys can pick up sound from right whales twenty-four hours a day, or when the weather's bad—times when planes aren't able to observe them, not to mention the times when the whales are underwater." —Anna Moscrop, International Fund for Animal Welfare

showed clear sounds by the mother during mother-calf reunions when they'd been separated, but when they were together they were extremely quiet, possibly to avoid drawing attention of predators or other whales, to protect the calf."

Imagine flying over the ocean, looking down. You'd see the whole thing, wouldn't you? *Hardly.*

You can't judge a whale by the tip of its tail.

A shark is much more than a pointed fin.

A periscope is just a peep of a submarine.

Setting your sails "wing and wing" makes your boat look like a bird.

Containers on a ship's deck are as mysterious as presents.

And you'll be lucky if you see a turtle at all.

The surface of the sea is like the cover of a book. Bright. Beautiful. But . . . it takes much more than a look to get to the heart of a book.

In 1978 Bill Haxby used satellite data to make the first computer map of the land under the ocean. The highest mountains in the North Atlantic are in the Mid-Atlantic Ridge. The satellite *Seasat* used microwaves instead of sound pulses to map the ocean floor.

Yes, they're the same microwaves as in an oven. In an oven they're more focused. In the ocean, they're not as intense—and aren't dangerous.

The ocean floor has as many hills and dales as the land. And, just as there are muskrats in the marshes, wolves on the plains, and bears in the mountains, different creatures live in the cliffs, peaks, canyons, and ravines of the ocean.

What's down there?

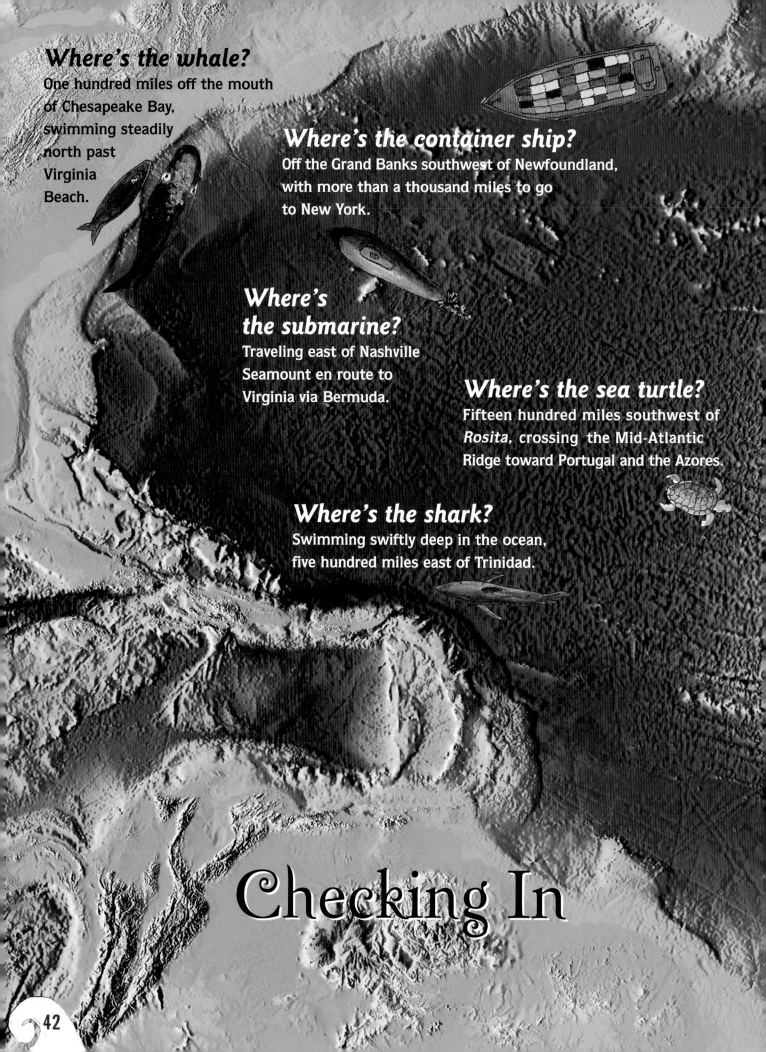

Where's the whale?
One hundred miles off the mouth of Chesapeake Bay, swimming steadily north past Virginia Beach.

Where's the container ship?
Off the Grand Banks southwest of Newfoundland, with more than a thousand miles to go to New York.

Where's the submarine?
Traveling east of Nashville Seamount en route to Virginia via Bermuda.

Where's the sea turtle?
Fifteen hundred miles southwest of *Rosita*, crossing the Mid-Atlantic Ridge toward Portugal and the Azores.

Where's the shark?
Swimming swiftly deep in the ocean, five hundred miles east of Trinidad.

Checking In

Where's the sailboat?
Setting a course
for Ireland.

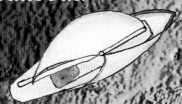

*J*ust off the beach, there's a place that has been explored much less than the surface of the moon. Every ocean scientist in the world daydreams about what it's like down there—and now they're putting their heads together to get a more complete view than ever before.

From 2003 to 2013, teams of scientists from a hundred groups in twenty countries will study what lives in different parts of the ocean. They're taking the Census of Marine Life (COML).

- Divers will visit canyons, seamounts (sea mountains), and ocean vents.

- Probes and drills will take samples of Arctic ice, deep sea sand, and sea water from the surface. Samples contain many known and unknown organisms.

- Artists will ride in submarines into the Mid-Atlantic Ridge to do paintings of the scenery there so landlubbers can see it.

- Satellite tags will monitor where turtles, whales, tuna, and lobsters—yes, lobsters!—go and what they do.

- And more! (For the latest, visit coml.org)

What's down there? I am!

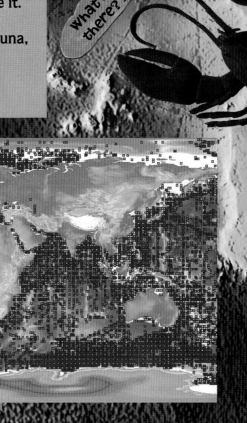

Each square on this map shows a place Census of Marine Life has data on. It's not just about depth, it's about what's down there.... But how do we get down there?

43

Submarine

submarine=under the sea

Where to?
Around the world.

What for?
To dive, surface, travel, scan, map, explore, protect, study.

Why do that?
Top secret!

What makes a tuna tick?

Tuna swim far and fast. When sub designers wanted to change their subs to make them go farther on fuel, they turned to tuna. Scientists at Massachusetts Institute of Technology built the robotuna to study how a tuna's shape and the way it moved made it speed so smoothly through the water.

The background of these pages shows the nuclear submarine USS Chicago at periscope depth.

What's down there?

Dancing crabs and mermaids? Since time began, people have dreamed and wondered what secrets the ocean floor held. But how could they get there to find out?

A boat on the surface, like a hiker in the woods, travels in two dimensions: east-west or north-south.

A bird, plane, squid, or sub uses a third dimension: up-down.

It's dark at the bottom of the ocean. How do you know where you are if you can't see? Like whales and dolphins, submarines use sound. Sound lets them figure their distance to the bottom of the ocean—their *altitude*. A sub matches its altitude with altitudes on a map of the ocean floor to find its position. The maps are built on top-secret information gathered by ships and subs over many years. Why keep the ocean floor secret? So enemy ships can't find *us*.

Who you callin' a tunatick?

44

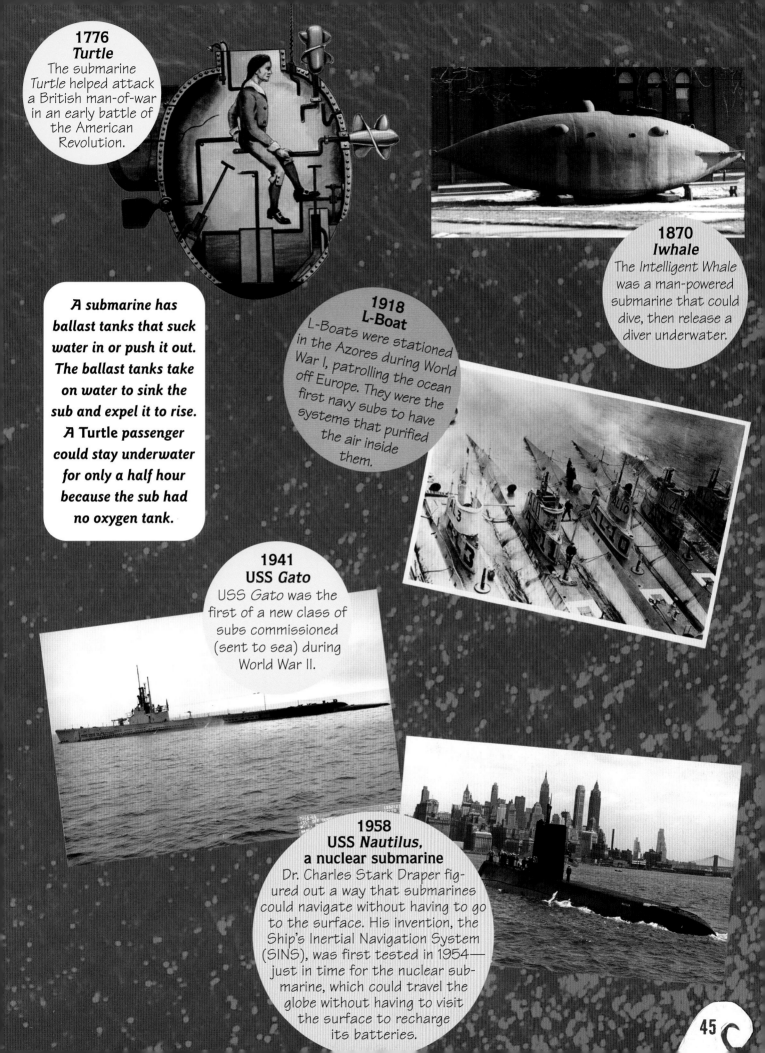

1776
Turtle
The submarine *Turtle* helped attack a British man-of-war in an early battle of the American Revolution.

1870
Iwhale
The *Intelligent Whale* was a man-powered submarine that could dive, then release a diver underwater.

A submarine has ballast tanks that suck water in or push it out. The ballast tanks take on water to sink the sub and expel it to rise. A Turtle passenger could stay underwater for only a half hour because the sub had no oxygen tank.

1918
L-Boat
L-Boats were stationed in the Azores during World War I, patrolling the ocean off Europe. They were the first navy subs to have systems that purified the air inside them.

1941
USS *Gato*
USS *Gato* was the first of a new class of subs commissioned (sent to sea) during World War II.

1958
USS *Nautilus*,
a nuclear submarine
Dr. Charles Stark Draper figured out a way that submarines could navigate without having to go to the surface. His invention, the Ship's Inertial Navigation System (SINS), was first tested in 1954—just in time for the nuclear submarine, which could travel the globe without having to visit the surface to recharge its batteries.

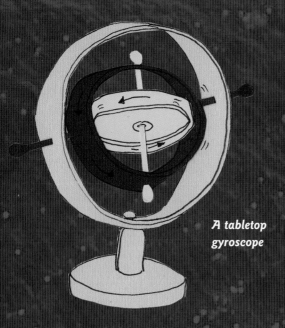

A tabletop gyroscope

- Gyroscopes check changes in direction.
- Fathometers check changes in the depth of the ocean.
- Accelerometers check changes in speed.
- The log keeps track of distance traveled.
- GPS gives position at the surface.
- Sextants back up GPS, just in case.
- Computers—and humans!—correct the course.

Submarines can use compasses, GPS, radar, and radios at the surface, but underwater, compasses and instruments that rely on sound waves traveling through the air don't work. Gyroscopes help keep the sub on track. When you spin a gyroscope on a table on land, its axle keeps pointing in the same direction. If you set the gyroscope on a table on a ship, the angle of the axle would change with the ship's movement. The gyroscope needs *gimbals*—supports that do the tilting so the axle stays oriented no matter what the ship does. Gimbals make the gyroscope a terrific compass.

Gyroscopes are the key to navigating the space shuttle, space station, and airplanes, too. Gyroscopes don't fight gravity; they just aren't affected by it. This is what makes them vital navigation tools. Gyroscopes seem mysterious; you can do a Web search to learn more about the phenomenon that rules them, called *precession,* or to see a video demonstration of how they work.

Submariners use inertial navigation systems to keep track of their position and course. An INS has two gyroscopes that work together to keep a sort of miniature table still (inert) no matter which way the gimbals turn. The result is that a sub's navigator can tell where the sub is and where it's going in three dimensions.

Inertial navigation systems, nuclear power, and computers have combined to create submarines that can go thousands of miles without coming up and without losing their way. But INS is the grandfather of modern navigation systems. Today the newest nuclear submarines plan their courses with Ring Laser Gyro Navigator (RLGN), a system of mirrors, lasers, and computers.

Before the 2000s, sub navigators spent a lot of time updating their charts—paper or digital—to reflect the changing location of buoys in the sea. Every few weeks, they had to "move" thousands of buoys to get an accurate picture of their position in the ocean. Now, instead of using paper charts, sub navigators are adopting digital chart systems.

These systems use computers and satellites. Navigators can simply pop up the sub's antennas and download changes via satellite signal from the Internet—and their computers will adjust their courses.

The system is far from perfect. In early 2005, USS *San Francisco* hit a seamount in the Caroline Islands in the Pacific Ocean. A Navy investigation found that some charts showed an area of "muddy water" where a seamount might be—but the chart in use showed nothing. The navigators were faulted for not comparing the depth data from their fathometer with the chart.

The USS Ohio in dry dock, being converted from a ballistic missile submarine to a guided missile submarine that launches Tomahawk missiles.

Built to Find a Target

Nuclear submarines are military vessels that can fire missiles or torpedoes. Missiles fly through the air; torpedoes go underwater. A torpedo stays attached to the sub by a thin wire that the sub cuts once the torpedo nears its target. After the torpedo is launched, course changes are sent through the wire from the sub. After the wire is cut, the torpedo uses active sonar to aim until it hits its target.

Missiles burst through the surface and fly off into the sky. While in the sub, they are programmed with a starting global position, and a course is calculated from that point. Tomahawk missiles, the "smartest" missiles, use their GPS systems to correct their own courses and home in on a target.

North Pole

The North Atlantic Ocean borders on the Arctic Circle. The ice cap at the North Pole is a frozen ocean of ice up to three thousand miles wide. Nuclear submarines traverse the Arctic Ocean by steaming under the ice. In 1958 the *Nautilus* became the first nuclear-powered submarine to cross the North Pole under the ice.

The crew of the USS L. Mendel Rivers *visits the North Pole*

The sub carried a team of researchers studying the ice thickness and the ocean under the ice. The researchers and crew got to see more of the Arctic than they expected.

Paul Beach, assistant navigator on the USS *L. Mendel Rivers,* knew that gyroscopes lost their accuracy at the North Pole, but he didn't expect to lose the ship's navigation system—Dual Miniature Inertial Navigation System, DMINS for short. When it was time for the sub to dive from the North Pole, Beach realized he had a problem.

"We were at the top of the world, at the North Pole. There are plenty of maps, but because we were straight north, our navigation system failed. INS has to refer its gyroscopes to something to align itself—and tried to find its angle to Polaris, the North Star. Well, at the North Pole, Polaris is straight up. DMINS didn't like it. Where's south? In all directions. It would not compute! The ship was left surfaced at the North Pole with no compass to guide it. We had to resort to more creative methods.

"I said to the captain, 'You've got to get me away from the North Pole to make it work.' We did two things. One, we figured the direction the nose of the boat was pointing. There's no course

at the North Pole; you're just heading down a longitude line, choosing which way to go as you're going to fall off the top of the world. I used a sextant to sight the moon. Then I used GPS at the stern and the bow, and set a course (based on these measurements). We 'pulled the cork,' sank and drove.

"The biggest challenge was keeping the boat pointed in a straight line. You use sonar to keep a record of the ship's noise. If the sound bends to the right or left, it means we're turning. We drove that way for eighteen hours, saying a prayer. We went 180 miles. The moment of truth had come.

"We popped up [through the ice] and got a GPS fix. We were on the right latitude line *to the mile,* but were on the wrong longitude line. We were 145 miles east of where we thought we were."

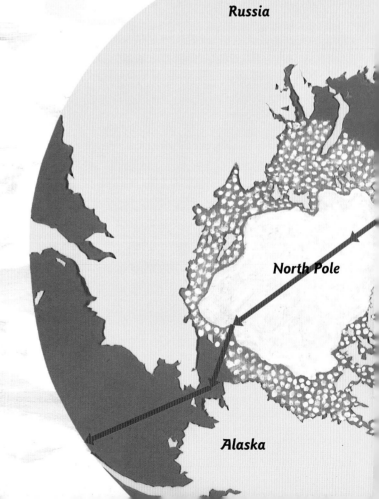

Russia

North Pole

Alaska

Just in case: the sail (the conning tower of a nuclear submarine) contains traditional, lower-tech navigational tools to back up INS, GPS, and sonar plotting. A sextant (for taking sights through the periscope when the sub nears the surface) and *Nautical Almanac* are handy, along with a chronometer to keep track of longitude. The sail also holds radio and radar antennas and a snorkel, which lets the sub "breathe"—take in fresh air and let out recycled air.

"Sailing under ice is never routine. There is and always will be an added element of danger."
—Dr. William M. Leary, *Under Ice: Waldo Lyon and the Invention of the Arctic Submarine*

333.34 -08.10 27APR03 01:05:35.10   6X 023

Subs come up where the ice is thinnest, and their crews never know what polar natives they'll meet. This polar bear is investigating the rudder of the USS Connecticut, as seen through the sub's periscope.

Vertical Navigation

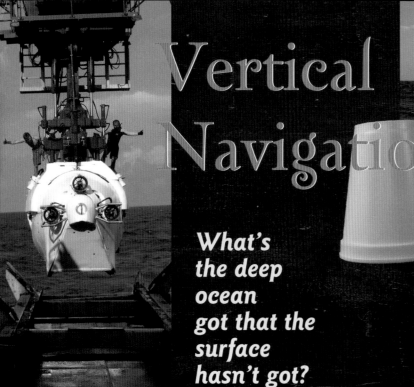

What's the deep ocean got that the surface hasn't got? A lot.

Alvin is a submarine big enough to hold three people, and is specially equipped to deal with the pressure at the ocean floor in the areas where ocean vents might be. *Alvin* continues to take researchers down to the ocean floor today. Dr. Craig Cary is one scientist who has made big discoveries in *Alvin.*

Alvin opened a new area of scientific discovery, and new submarines—and submarine-type vehicles—have been developed to help scientists, including a new *Alvin* in the works. *Alvin* is a deep submergence vehicle (DSV). It can drive itself; it isn't attached to anything or controlled by anything. However, *Alvin* does receive navigation directions from the mother ship, Research Vessel *Atlantis,* that carries it out to the place in the ocean where scientists want to dive.

- *Jason II/Medea* is a remotely operated vehicle (ROV) that *Alvin's* pilot can control. *Jason II/Medea* has a mechanical hand that can gather samples or move things.
- *Argo II* is a video camera robot that sends pictures back to a mother ship through a fiberoptic cable.
- And ABE, the Autonomous Benthic Explorer, can dive by itself. Its instruments gather information that is used to make detailed maps of the ocean floor. ABE can be sent ahead of *Alvin* as a "scout" to see what the ocean floor is like.

How deep can you go?

Alvin can sink as deep as 14,764 feet (4,500m). Most of *Alvin's* nearly four thousand dives have not been that deep. *Alvin II* will be able to dive deeper—up to 21,326 feet (6,500m).

The deepest dive was 35,810 feet (10,915m). It was made in a *bathyscaphe* sub called *Trieste* in 1960. *Trieste* dove to the bottom of the Marianas Trench off Guam.

As you descend through the ocean's levels, the water pressure grows. *Alvin* sinks a hundred meters a minute. With every ten meters, the water pressure increases one *atmosphere.* This measurement is called an atmosphere because it is equivalent to the pressure of Earth's whole atmosphere weighing down on Earth.

The deepest ocean, with the entire sea pressing down on it, reaches 250 atmospheres of pressure. Creatures that live there are specially adapted to pressure and cold and darkness. But humans can't survive without the controlled environment of a submarine.

Dr. Craig Cary is a University of Delaware biologist who studies Pompeii worms, which live in the almost-boiling-hot water around undersea vents. To do his research, he descends to the ocean floor in *Alvin.*

"Once you leave the surface, it starts to get dark quite rapidly," Craig says. "You can see the color change as it gets dark. It turns into this very blue color." The descent to the seafloor takes two hours.

"The ship always 'knows' where *Alvin* is better than *Alvin* knows itself," says Craig. He describes how this works. The ship drops down two sonar pingers, which rest on the bottom and send out their signals. This gives the ship's navigator a grid into which *Alvin* drops. Based on the sonar and the ship's GPS, navigators figure out what instructions to give the *Alvin* pilot. "Say *Alvin* goes into a gully and can't 'hear' the pinger," suggests Craig. "The ship can always find *Alvin*'s position and give it directions."

Those directions might sound something like this: "*Alvin*, this is *Atlantis.* Your target is at 145°. Slow to forty amps and proceed at that speed for ten minutes."

Near bottom, *Alvin* drops some of its weights and pumps water out. The aim is *neutral buoyancy*, neither sinking nor rising. This lets *Alvin* "fly" like a helicopter scanning the terrain below.

Tube worms and vent crabs live at the ocean vents.

The Pompeii worm (named for the famous town in Italy that was destroyed by a volcanic eruption) can live in temperatures up to 176° F. Craig Cary thinks its secret is the gray fuzzy bacteria on its back.

Alvin *did it*

- found a hydrogen bomb lost when a plane crashed
- was lost on the sea bottom (unmanned) for eight months
- explored the Mid-Atlantic Ridge, the Galapagos Rift, the Cayman Trough, and the East Pacific Rise
- visited wreck of the Titanic and other wrecks
- changed the way oceanographers study the ocean

In 1977 Alvin scientists first found life in hydrothermal vents, cracks in the ocean floor that spew out poisonous chemicals and sizzling hot water boiled by the heat coming from Earth's core. Steamy, toxic, and miles from surface sunshine, vents are hotbeds of wildlife:

- GIANT CLAMS twelve inches long!
- THE GARDEN OF EDEN, where tube worms host a whole food chain of creatures that live on hydrogen sulfide and never see the SUN!
- CHIMNEYS of hardened minerals from Earth's molten core! They are home to microscopic animals that live nowhere else on earth!

The picture above shows Alvin, some chimneys, giant clams, vent crabs, and tube worms as they would look if there were some light on the subject. But the only light so deep comes from Alvin. Vents are found by towing a temperature sensor—a thermometer that beeps the instant the temperature rises a thousandth of a degree. Sonar guides a camera towed fifteen feet from the bottom. This way researchers pinpoint areas they want to explore.

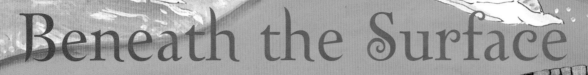

Beneath the Surface

Epipelagic zone:
from the surface to 450 feet down

Little fish by the millions school to the surface to eat plankton; bigger fish follow them there.

Mesopelagic zone:
450 to 3,300 feet down

At night the world's biggest migration takes place. More animals travel farther then than in the day. This is when jellyfish come up to the ocean's surface to eat the plankton that have been making sunlight into food all day. Larger fish come to eat the jellies, and humans may set out lines or nets to catch the fish. In the morning the fishermen haul in their catch. The fish have moved down, and moved on. The jellies sink again, and the plankton soak up the light once more.

When night falls, the great vertical migration begins anew.

Sunlight reaches 450 feet into the ocean. Water above this level is crystal blue. Water below it grows dim and murky as you sink deeper. What sinks deeper? A submarine, for one. Research robot subs drop down on tethers and send video and still pictures back to ships on the surface.

1. sea turtle	15. goby
2. sailboat	16. sunfish
3. container ship	17. ctenophore
4. right whale mother and calf	18. gag
	19. amberjack
5. shark	20. jelly
6. submarine	21. jelly
7. krill	22. blowfish
8. sea cucumber	23. acantharean
9. flying fish	24. anglerfish
10. pencil urchin	25. vent crab
11. squid	26. tube worm
12. barracuda	27. red anemone
13. Atlantic herring	28. sun star
14. sea butterfly	29. diatom

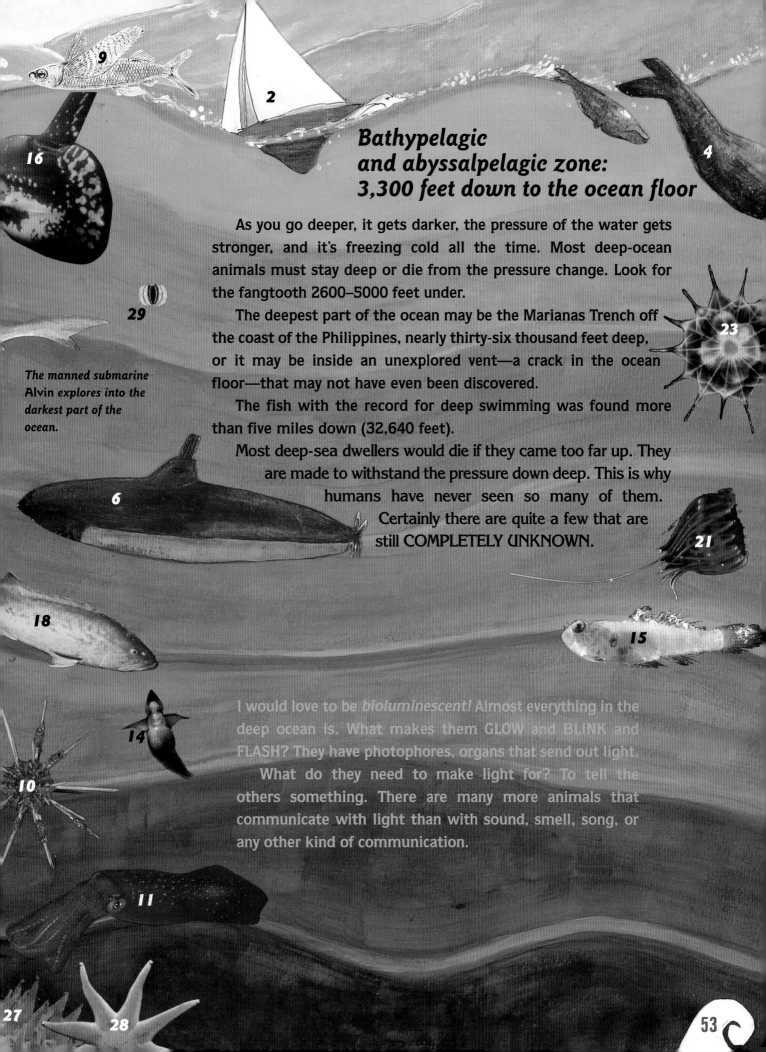

Bathypelagic and abyssalpelagic zone: 3,300 feet down to the ocean floor

As you go deeper, it gets darker, the pressure of the water gets stronger, and it's freezing cold all the time. Most deep-ocean animals must stay deep or die from the pressure change. Look for the fangtooth 2600–5000 feet under.

The deepest part of the ocean may be the Marianas Trench off the coast of the Philippines, nearly thirty-six thousand feet deep, or it may be inside an unexplored vent—a crack in the ocean floor—that may not have even been discovered.

The fish with the record for deep swimming was found more than five miles down (32,640 feet).

Most deep-sea dwellers would die if they came too far up. They are made to withstand the pressure down deep. This is why humans have never seen so many of them. Certainly there are quite a few that are still COMPLETELY UNKNOWN.

The manned submarine Alvin *explores into the darkest part of the ocean.*

I would love to be *bioluminescent!* Almost everything in the deep ocean is. What makes them GLOW and BLINK and FLASH? They have photophores, organs that send out light.

What do they need to make light for? To tell the others something. There are many more animals that communicate with light than with sound, smell, song, or any other kind of communication.

Blue shark (Prionace glauca)

A Shark's Schedule of Events

May, June, and July: Blue sharks breed along the New England continental shelf and slope waters.

August, September: Female blue sharks swim away from the shelf, heading east.

Spring: Females pup off the coasts of Spain and North Africa before beginning the swim west. No one is sure what male sharks do after breeding; they are less predictable, says shark researcher Chris McNally.

Where to?

Blue sharks tagged in the U.S. and in Ireland (maps on facing page) make giant journeys across the wide ocean.

What for?

Built for speed *and* distance, the blue shark moves like a dart in quest of squid, mackerel, cod, tuna, octopus, and other sharks.

Why do that?

1. Sharks swim north or south as the season changes to stay with the water temperature they "like."
2. Sharks move inshore or offshore, north or south, to find their mating grounds and breeding grounds.
3. Sharks follow the fish they eat.

When students at St. George's School in Middletown, Rhode Island, play tag, blue sharks are It. The kids go to sea on the school's research vessel, SSV *Geronimo*, to catch and tag blue sharks in a program that began in 1974 and continues today. The map on page 55 includes some of the St. George's School sharks. Tagged off Rhode Island, blue sharks take off across the Atlantic on loops that keep them near the schools of fish that follow the North Atlantic gyre, the current—an ocean river—that sweeps clockwise. (The Gulf Stream is part of the North Atlantic gyre.)

The sharks tagged by *Geronimo* are often caught not far away, as "bycatch" of swordfish and tuna fishermen working on the Grand Banks off the coast of Newfoundland.

Male blue sharks have been observed "hanging out" at the seamounts in the middle of the western Atlantic. *Seamounts* are undersea mountains whose slopes create "upwelling"—flows of cold water that rise up from the ocean floor. This upwelling gives rise to lots of food fish—and so, to sharks.

Randy Kochevar, a biologist studying blue sharks in the Pacific, says, "If you looked at a terrestrial [land] environment and found animals congregating around a water hole, the reason would be obvious: they're attracted to the water."

In the ocean we don't know what drives the formation of a "hot spot" (a place where sharks and other animals congregate). Is it the lay of the land—such as seamounts? Is it current or temperature? "Finding the answer is very difficult, because the factors are invisible," says Randy. "We can't *see* what makes the shark go right or left, to shallower or deeper water."

So shark scientists tag sharks and overlay their routes with oceanographic data, such as wave height at the surface, temperature, salinity, and so on. They're looking at a pattern that shows them more about what sharks want.

Sharks tagged on one side of the Atlantic and recaptured weeks, months, or years later on the other side are helping us solve the mysteries of shark migration.

- Sharks have been around for 400 million years.
- Like some dinosaurs, which were also alive 400 million years ago, prehistoric sharks were huge: up to eighty feet long!
- Experts figure that more than 100 million sharks and shark-like fish such as skates and rays are killed each year.

Sharks attack sixty to eighty people each year, and about a dozen people die as a result.

"We have this idea of sharks being really fierce predators—and they are. They're at the top of the food chain. But they're also really fragile." Julia K. Baum of Dalhousie University, Halifax, Nova Scotia, is the lead author of a study of Atlantic sharks that showed that the number of sharks dropped dramatically because of fishing. Blue shark populations fell 60 percent between 1986 and 2000.

Julia says that the only thing that will help the shark numbers rise again is less fishing. Because sharks go after the same fish that fishermen do, they often get caught in their nets and on their lines. Julia Baum's team used fishing records—the fishing boats' logbooks—to find out how shark populations change.

"The experience of tagging is hard work. First you have to catch the shark on rod and line and then tag and release as quickly as possible. Skippers and anglers alike get great satisfaction in witnessing a tagged blue shark swimming away from the boat."—Peter Green, Central Fisheries Board of Ireland

R/V GERONIMO BLUE SHARK TAG RETURNS

UNITED STATES
EUROPE
AFRICA
SOUTH AMERICA

Blue Shark Recaptures

New Foundland (23)
Long Is. (8)
Azores (350)
Gulf of Mexico (1)
Barbados (5)
Canaries (60)
Cape Verde Is. (20)
(1)
(3)
(5)
(2)
Equator

NOS. TAGGED TO DEC. '98:	15037
NOS. RECAPTURED TO DEC. '98	490

DAYS AT LIBERTY	2 - 1419
DISTANCE TRAVELLED	0 - 4250
RECAPTURE RATE	3.25%

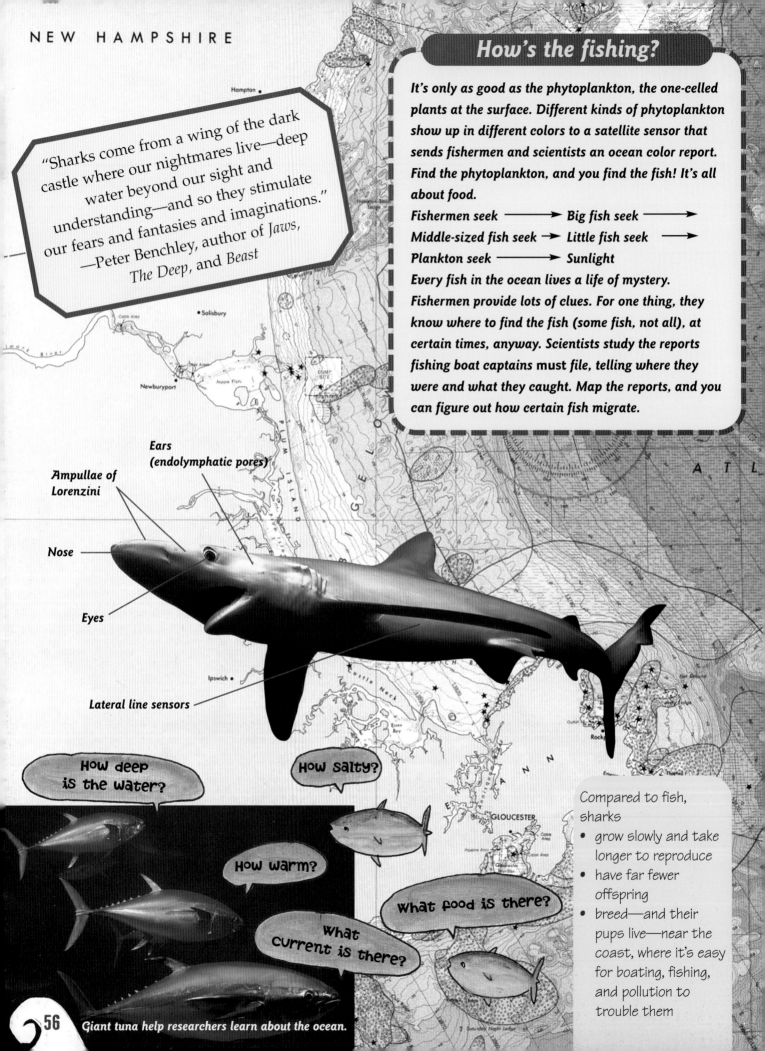

How's the fishing?

It's only as good as the phytoplankton, the one-celled plants at the surface. Different kinds of phytoplankton show up in different colors to a satellite sensor that sends fishermen and scientists an ocean color report. Find the phytoplankton, and you find the fish! It's all about food.

Fishermen seek ⟶ Big fish seek ⟶

Middle-sized fish seek → Little fish seek ⟶

Plankton seek ⟶ Sunlight

Every fish in the ocean lives a life of mystery. Fishermen provide lots of clues. For one thing, they know where to find the fish (some fish, not all), at certain times, anyway. Scientists study the reports fishing boat captains must file, telling where they were and what they caught. Map the reports, and you can figure out how certain fish migrate.

"Sharks come from a wing of the dark castle where our nightmares live—deep water beyond our sight and understanding—and so they stimulate our fears and fantasies and imaginations."
—Peter Benchley, author of *Jaws*, *The Deep*, and *Beast*

Ears
(endolymphatic pores)

Ampullae of
Lorenzini

Nose

Eyes

Lateral line sensors

How deep
is the water?

How salty?

How warm?

What
current is there?

What food is there?

Compared to fish, sharks
- grow slowly and take longer to reproduce
- have far fewer offspring
- breed—and their pups live—near the coast, where it's easy for boating, fishing, and pollution to trouble them

56 *Giant tuna help researchers learn about the ocean.*

On the Trail of Sharks

Eyes: Color vision is seven times as good as a human's.
Nose: Blue sharks can smell one drop of blood in one million drops of water. They can smell blood a quarter of a mile away.
Ears (endolymphatic pores): Sharks can hear low-frequency sounds and can tell which direction a sound comes from.

Fish (bony fishes) and sharks (fish with skeletons made of cartilage, not bone) have different life cycles. Although more fish than sharks are caught, fish are much quicker to replace themselves.

Blue sharks need the water they swim in to be from 45° to 65° Fahrenheit. One reason they migrate from one side of the ocean to the other is to stick with fish that live in those temperatures. Blue sharks also migrate vertically to find the right temperature, swimming in deeper water as they near the equator, staying close to the surface as they move toward the poles. In places where the continental shelf hugs the shore, blue sharks will go closer to the coast as water cools at night, then out to sea at dawn.

Tiny changes in temperature can cause electrical changes in a shark's body, helping it to respond lightning-quick. The tiny ampullae—gel-filled canals in the snout—allow sharks to detect electrical fields created by other animals, including prey. A research experiment found that blue sharks could detect the heartbeat of a fish in a water-filled plastic box buried in sand.

Sharks never stop. They keep on moving in order to keep on living. Fish have swim bladders, special organs that keep them afloat whether or not they swim. Sharks don't have swim bladders, so they sink if they stop swimming.

Swordfish and tuna fishermen keep careful watch on the temperature of the ocean they fish in, because the fish, like blue sharks, prefer a precise temperature. "Stay away from the blue dogs," a veteran fisherman will tell a beginner. "Blue dogs" is the nickname for blue sharks, which prefer water a tad cooler than tuna and swordfish do.

Some tuna crossed the Pacific in just twenty-one days. Blue sharks are speedy, too. The fastest sharks achieve speed bursts of more than 40 mph.

Barbara Block of Stanford University and Molly Lutcavage of the University of New Hampshire tag giant tuna with pop-up tags. Barbara says it's as if the tuna become robots, swimming around the ocean taking water samples and collecting data that will tell us more about them and about the ocean they—and blue sharks—swim in.

Currents and Weather

This map shows sea surface temperature. Areas in black could not be viewed by the satellite.

Pentad 2004/07/29-2004/08/02

It could be as far off as a thin wisp of gray cloud on the horizon, spied by a wary fisherman along the Florida coast. The fisherman pulls her lines from the water and misses catching a blue shark.

It could be as vague as the ache in the knee of a crew member on a container ship off Bermuda. He doesn't complain, and the ship sticks to its course to New York.

It could be as clear as a sudden wave that washes over the head of the turtle and sends it toward Davy Jones's locker.

It could be as distant as a message from a satellite to a navigator in a nuclear submarine.

It could be as close to home as a stomach-churning swell that makes a sailor think, "Uh-oh."

Who knows what the whale thinks? It could be that she realizes her baby can't dive for as long as she can . . . and wonders how he'll weather the storm.

What makes the currents?
The winds do.

What makes the wind?
The earth's rotation and the warming action of the sun.

Every ocean has prevailing winds—major winds that   blow in one direction—as well as minor winds that switch around, depending on seasons, storms, and other weather. The Pacific and Atlantic both have strong prevailing winds called *trade winds*, at 30°N and 30°S. Trade winds were named by sailors on trade ships who appreciated the extra help their ships got when they sailed in the direction the winds were blowing—not just because the wind pushed them, but also because they could ride the ocean current in the direction they wanted to go.

On a plane or ship anywhere in the Northern Hemisphere, the trip from west to east goes more quickly and takes less fuel than a trip from east to west. In the Southern Hemisphere, it's easier to go east to west.

Hurricane season in the North Atlantic lasts from May to October, with the biggest threat coming at the end of the season, from August on.

Winds up to 150 miles per hour swirl across the sky and whip the ocean into a churning mixing bowl. When shore dwellers get the good news that a storm has gone out to sea, that's when the plot thickens for travelers at sea. Fishing boats, container ships, and other vessels crossing the ocean are too far from shore for Coast Guard res-

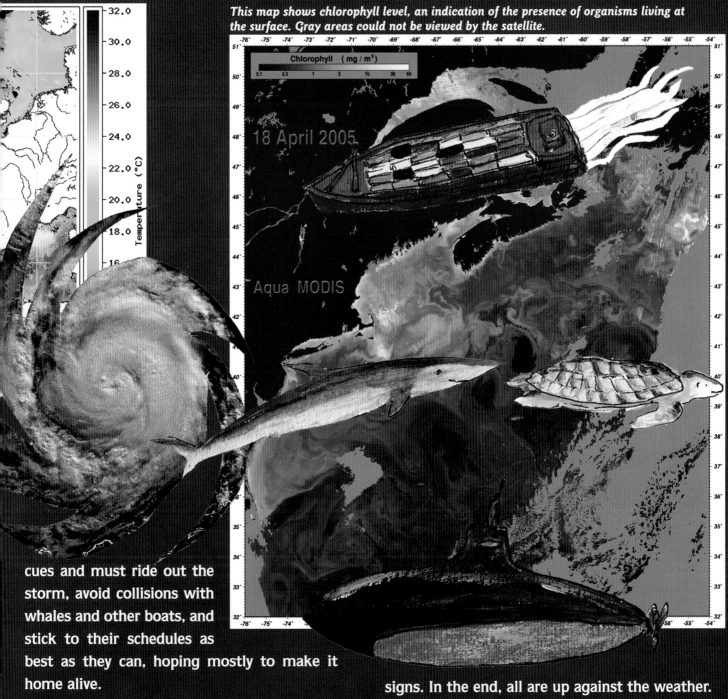

Chlorophyll (mg / m³)

0.1   0.3   1   3   10   30   60

18 April 2005

Aqua MODIS

Temperature (°C)

32.0
30.0
28.0
26.0
24.0
22.0
20.0
18.0
16.0

cues and must ride out the storm, avoid collisions with whales and other boats, and stick to their schedules as best as they can, hoping mostly to make it home alive.

What's the weather where you are?

Ships, subs, and sailboats get satellite or radio reports of wind, sea surface temperature, and weather predictions. Weather faxes help, too. The map on page 58 shows sea surface temperature across the ocean. By knowing sea surface temperature, you can trace the Gulf Stream in yellow, note the coldest areas of the ocean, and predict weather patterns. Sharks, whales, and turtles— and people, to be sure—use their senses to tune in to the increases in wind, the drop in pressure, changes in the clouds and temperature, and other

signs. In the end, all are up against the weather.

Things on the surface are most at risk.

Sharks and subs can dive, staying below for the duration of the hurricane. What about a whale that needs to come to the surface to breathe?

Sailboats and container ships may turn their noses to the wind, a steady position for riding out a storm—though some argue that it's better to run before the wind, rather than turning against it. *Rosita* uses her rudder and, sometimes, engine power, to face out a storm.

The sea turtle just swims, but, like all of them, may be blown off course, sunk by rogue waves, and possibly, lost.

Adrift

jetsam: things thrown into the sea

flotsam: things that fall into the sea

If TVs could float across the ocean and show us where they've been . . .

If somebody's lost glasses could drift to the shore and tell us what they'd seen . . .

What stories would these drifters tell?

Stories of jellyfish and plankton, sea slugs and dolphin fish, manta rays and basking sharks, lost fishing nets and Mylar balloons, sunfish and moonfish, sargassum weed and seahorses, man-o'-war tentacles and shark fins, flotsam and jetsam, crates lost by container ships and coconuts on a trip around the world on the waves.

> When Robin Lee Graham sailed the world, all along the way he tossed message bottles overboard. It takes a bottle about one hundred days to float across the Atlantic.

Drifters aren't just flotsam and jetsam. Drifters are instruments on buoys that float around the ocean, recording information about temperature, surface windspeed, currents, and the *salinity*—the saltiness—of the water. Phil Richardson of the Woods Hole Oceanographic Institution says, "Buoys show us where the water is going, where the water is coming from, and where it goes."

Phil began studying drift in the North Atlantic by tracing the trails of ships that were wrecked and abandoned at sea. These "ghost ships" floated along and were sighted by other ships, whose captains noted their positions. Phil created maps showing where the ghost ships drifted. He modified his maps based on data from drifter buoys to show how water moved through the Atlantic.

Drifter buoy data helps feed computer models of the ocean that show how certain events might change conditions. What sort of events? Tidal waves (tsunami). Earthquakes. Hurricanes. A rise in water levels that would occur if the polar ice melted. The path oil or sewage or chemicals might take if they were spilled or dumped in the ocean.

Scientists deploy (set up) drifters from ships or drop them from planes. The buoys have transmitters and use satellites to transfer data to the scientists' labs. Mayra Pazos of the National Oceanic and Atmospheric Administration (NOAA) Drifting Buoys Center in Miami says that the aim

The world's biggest fish, the whale shark, follows drifting plankton. One tagged whale shark traveled fourteen thousand miles in forty months. Whale sharks can grow up to fifty feet long (fifteen m).

In 1992 a shipment of twenty-nine thousand toy ducks, beavers, turtles, and fish fell from a container ship in the Pacific. OSCURS showed the toys would pass through the Arctic Circle and wash up along the East Coast of the U.S. beginning in summer 2003. There is still a hundred-dollar reward offered for any that are found.

is to have one buoy in every 5° latitude by 5° longitude square in the ocean. "Buoys can die or run aground," Mayra says, "so we deploy more each year." There are hundreds in the North Atlantic so far; Mayra says that 1,250 are needed. During 1998, drifters dropped into the ocean sent back their positions every six hours.

What's with the hockey equipment on these pages? The current is, that's what. Every year, although millions of containers carried by container ships arrive safely, a few fall off ships because of storms or high seas. In the 1990s a container holding eighty thousand sports shoes was lost. Identification numbers printed inside the shoes could be matched with shipping lists to show which ship had lost them.

Dr. Curt Ebbesmeyer, an oceanographer, used identification numbers like these to create a computer model of the currents of the Pacific Ocean. The model is called OSCURS, which stands for ocean surface current simulations. Curt got a call from a friend telling him when and where a shipment of hockey equipment had fallen from a ship. He put the data into the model and predicted which beach the equipment should wash

up on, and a date. That day he hit the beach, and as he walked he saw them: hockey gloves, shin guards. His model was right!

OSCURS shows that the current takes water all the way around the Pacific Ocean every seven years. The currents in the Atlantic are just as powerful. The Gulf Stream sweeps north from the Caribbean Sea, close to the Florida coast, follows the continental shelf up the U.S. coast, arcs out to sea past Cape Cod, then roars a hundred miles a day toward Portugal.

The Gulf Stream carries warm water into the North Atlantic, which is why Europe isn't as cold as other places at the same latitude. If the Gulf Stream weren't there, Ireland would be as frozen as the Arctic, and Europe would be so cold trees wouldn't grow.

The submarine Benjamin Franklin was designed to drift in the Gulf Stream, carried along by the current. On its first voyage, in 1964, it drifted for a month from Florida to Nova Scotia without coming up once.

Container Ship

Where to?
Everywhere!

What for?

To carry things from port to port.

Why do that?

So people can buy and sell goods.

Cargo in crates, barrels, and bundles used to be lifted in and out of ships' holds in huge slings. Shippers began using containers in 1958.

Ports and ships measure their business as the number of TEUs they handle. TEU stands for twenty-foot equivalent unit. For a long time, shipbuilders wouldn't make ships larger than

"panamax"—32.2 meters wide, the biggest size that could fit through the Panama Canal. Panamax ships carry more than four thousand TEU—about two thousand truck-sized containers. Post-panamax ships and the new post-panamax giants can carry much more. Shippers expect that by 2010, over thirty ships carrying more than nine thousand TEUs will hit the waves. They'll stick to seaports and routes that can accommodate their size and *draft*—how low they *draw*, or sink, when fully loaded. Ports such as New York Harbor must be dredged (deepened) to allow the super-ships to fit.

Many people are worried about the problems that container ships create: collisions with marine mammals, ship noise that could harm the ears of sea animals, pollution to air and water. The number of containers transported increases every year.

Container ships are, on average, the length of more than two football fields, and weigh from fifty thousand to a hundred thousand tons. They don't stop easily, and if they go slowly, especially in coastal areas, they can be swept aground by currents or tides.

Today almost all of the cargo transported

This map shows worldwide shipping routes, which make use of trade winds and ocean currents, while relying on ship power too, of course.

from one port to another travels in containers on fast-moving container ships. A ship can make the voyage from Hong Kong to New York in just seventeen days, and can cross the Atlantic in under a week. Container ships are equipped to navigate huge distances across the ocean. Quick Atlantic transits are great for transporting time-sensitive cargo like certain foods. Before GPS, this kind of speed wasn't possible.

The first GPS instruments for ocean navigation were offered in 1985. Now practically every ship carries them. Container ships rely on Differential Global Positioning Systems (DGPS), a highly detailed and specific version of GPS. DGPS interacts with ship communications to pinpoint the locations of ships in the ocean and their destinations. But container ships still stick to the shipping lanes established years ago—sometimes hundreds of years ago—because of the influence of the trade winds and currents.

In the past, navigators had to check several different radar viewers in order to get a complete look—and sometimes their view had blind spots. Now container ships get another boost from multimode navigational radar systems that put all the information they get into one view. Less possibility of error means—you guessed it—fewer accidents.

Between 1994 and 2005, the number of containers transported each year tripled from 322 million to 971 million metric tons!

Giant cranes hoist containers into stacks on the ships' decks—as fast as thirty an hour. The aim of the shippers is to spend the least possible time in port.

"A ship in a harbor is safe . . ."

For ships built to cross the ocean quickly, bays, channels, and harbors are tricky going. They have to rely on tugboats. Michael Moran, founder of Moran Towing, began his career as a mule driver on the Erie Canal. (Mules were the "tugboats" on barge canals, pulling the barges on long ropes.) Before tugboats had radios, Moran's dispatcher sat on a high ledge over New York Harbor. When a ship neared the harbor, the tug dispatchers competed to be the first to see it and send a tug to guide it in. It helped to have a big mouth, because the dispatchers yelled down to their tugs to get going (and told them where to go).

Tugboat dispatcher Kimberly Shelley watches tide and weather monitors, works two computers, handles twelve phone lines, and talks to her tugs on a VHS radio.

"Coming in from the sea buoy at 19:50 hours, a harbor pilot has just boarded the *Da He*. It's a Cosco ship from Hong Kong, a container ship 903 feet long, 135 feet above the water. Draft has been confirmed at 35 feet 6 inches. . . ."

Kimberly Shelley is a Moran dispatcher. She

makes sure tugs meet the ships, and she helps tug captains keep track of time and tide schedules in her home port of Charleston, South Carolina.

Q Is every ship the same?

A I must research each ship that comes in: how long it is, its *beam* (width), its *draft*, whether it's a tanker or container ship. You can't believe how big the ships are until you come up in a little tug.

Q How do you know a ship is coming?

A The shipping agent will call the pilot office to let us know when the ship will arrive at the Charleston Sea Buoy—an hour and forty-five minutes outside the harbor entrance. The sea pilot boards the ship there and brings it about ten miles in, to Buoy Six, where the harbor pilot and dock pilot board. They ride out to the ship on a tugboat, then climb up a rope ladder hung down the side of the ship—a dicey operation in bad weather or rough seas, and risky anytime.

Q What do you do next?

A I get my tugs ready. The docking pilot decides how many tugs to put with each ship. One night we might have a ship coming in as the tide is going out. Another ship may have a deep draft. A ship may need to turn around upon docking or sailing. Or the U.S. Coast Guard may order tug assistance if the ship has engine or steering problems. They may need extra tugs to keep the ship moving in the right direction and help it to stay in the channel so it doesn't run aground.

The docking pilot instructs the tugs from the very top of the ship's bridge, where he stands at the wheel with the captain.

A ship uses power all the way into the berth, the parking area with the crane that will unload and load it. The tug goes alongside and "makes up" to it—attaching a line to the ship. The ship lowers speed as it comes close to the berth, and continues to drop speed. The tugboat presses its rubber bumper right up against the ship, pushing the ship into place.

Q How do tugboat captains know where they're going?

A Imagine pushing a long chain of cargo barges as a heavy fog creeps around you, blinding you, hiding the shore and the other boats. New York tugboat navigators used to rely on radar, charts, and navigation by sight to guide their tugs through New York Harbor and the bays and rivers leading into it. Now tugboat navigators have added GPS and computer software to the mix. They rely on their hippocampus, too. They check the information on the high-tech instruments against what's visible out the window and—even more—against their mental map of what's under the water.

Buoys and gulls . . . help coast navigators!

Seamen are superstitious. Some listen to gut feelings—premonitions—at the dock and quit the crew . . . and some later learn that their ships went down. To be safe, many believe:

- *Don't set sail on a Friday.*
- *Don't paint your boat yellow.*
- *Don't let a pig on board or even say the word pig. (Pigs can't fly, and they can't swim, either.)*
- *Don't whistle into the wind or anywhere else at sea. It will bring strong winds and rough seas.*

" . . . but that is not what ships are for."

On the other side of the Atlantic, pilots continually guide ships through the Dover Straits in the English Channel between England and France. The Channel is chock-full of container ships, tankers, tugs, ferries, fishing boats, sailboats, and more. The pilot may board in ports such as LeHavre or Southampton, or may take a boat out to a ship, then climb a ladder to get aboard. He may also fly out in a helicopter. Think that sounds better than climbing the ladder? If the chopper can't land, the pilot is lowered to deck on a wire.

Captains of smaller ships are advised to learn to spot big ships in the dark or the fog. *All* ships are required to use running lights, with a green light to starboard (the right side) and a red light to port (the left). If you can see *both* lights, and the green is on your left, you're directly in the ship's path. Move fast!

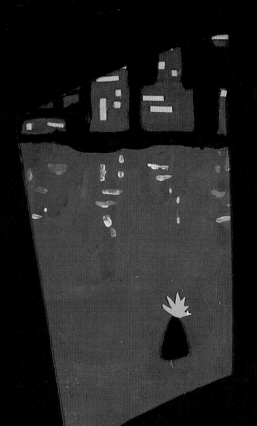

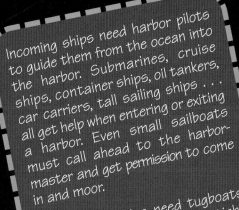

Incoming ships need harbor pilots to guide them from the ocean into the harbor. Submarines, cruise ships, container ships, oil tankers, car carriers, tall sailing ships . . . all get help when entering or exiting a harbor. Even small sailboats must call ahead to the harbormaster and get permission to come in and moor.

The biggest ships need tugboats to help them manage the tight corners and narrow passageways of the harbor. The tugboat may carry a docking pilot to the ship. The docking pilot's job is to steer the ship to the dock and stay with it until all is secure.

A pilot climbs from a tiny launch up the stern of an enormous container ship outside the harbor at Charleston, South Carolina.

Chris Moore mans the helm of *Rosita* on a gray day.

Heavy Seas Ahead!

A boat's anemometer (at right) shows a maximum wind speed of 120 mph. In a hurricane the anemometer may seem "stuck" at the high point, while a barometer, which measures the pressure of the atmosphere, plummets as the storm nears.

One of the biggest dangers to ships on the high seas is bad weather. The National Weather Service helps ships help themselves. As part of their regular satellite ship-to-shore communications, container ships use their instruments to

Water-proof gear is important on a sailboat.

23:39 barometer 987.5 mb, wind NE at 120 mph. Almost midnight, and the instruments indicate fierce, dirty weather.

make reports about the sea, sky, clouds, and other conditions. These in turn are used to keep other ships informed, and to track weather that might turn toward the land.

What happens to container ships

in port if there's a storm, as there often is along the coast of the Carolinas? Kimberly Shelley says, "If they're in port they might try to get *out*, where they can ride out the storm without worrying about hitting much of anything. They may go up a river, inland, or just be secured with extra lines."

Where should a sub be in a storm?

In hurricanes, submarines can often be found steaming out to sea, where they can dive and stay under the bad weather. Why not stay in port? Wind and waves can bang up the sub *and* its pier. Instead, sub crews go into emergency mode getting ready to go to sea.

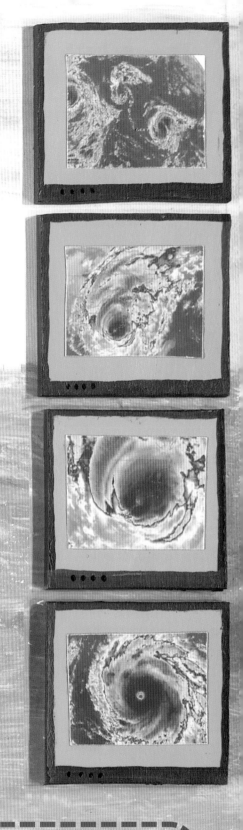

The maps on the TVs are computer weather maps from the GOES-8 satellite.

Batten down the hatches! Swirling hurricanes, born from a powerful mix of warm and cool wind over the ocean, are bad news for land and sea.

"Get off that boat!"

That's what the crew of a sailboat might hear over the radio during a hurricane. They can tune their radios to Hurricane Net and can watch the atmospheric pressure readings on their barometer and the wind speed on their anemometer.

Mammoth hurricanes have wind speeds over 135 mph. But that's *sustained*, or continuous wind. A category five hurricane (like Hurricane Hugo, which swept through the Carolinas in 1998) has *gusts* (sudden winds) of up to 175–200 mph.

In a hurricane even ships in harbor may easily be ripped off their anchors or moorings and be wrecked. Some wash onto shore. Boats close to shore may head up rivers or into bays for sheltered waters—but rising tides and storm surges can threaten them inland, too. In 2006, a year after Hurricane Katrina, wrecked shrimp boats still sat in inland meadows.

What if you're on a ship far out at sea? As a safety measure, ships report their positions to the U.S. Coast Guard's Automated Mutual Assistance Vessel Rescue system (AMVER). Coast Guard helicopters can fly only two hundred miles from land; beyond that they won't have enough fuel to make it back. If your boat or ship gets into trouble farther out, you can call AMVER. The system gets in touch with ships that might be near you and can send them to help.

What do animals do in a storm?

Scientists think lost or disoriented whales may beach themselves. But storms don't seem to cause most whales to get lost. Their navigational skills must take over. Whether they use Earth's magnetic field or the stars, moon, and sun or messages in whales' songs, whales usually figure things out and get where they're going just fine, even in the roughest, most dangerous seas.

While hurricanes aren't especially dangerous to sharks, sharks can be more dangerous to people because of hurricanes. George Burgess of the International Shark Attack File reports that shark attacks on swimmers and surfers rise during and after hurricanes. That's because hurricanes stir up sand from the bottom, making the water murky—and sharks can mistake people for fish. Out in the open sea, blue sharks, like subs, can dive below the worst of the weather.

In 1999 Hurricane Irene washed away half the sea turtle nests on North Carolina beaches. Heavier, older turtles may be able to fight the strong currents, but smaller surface swimmers are sometimes lost or thrown off course.

In a storm, waves seem higher than mountains.

Man Overboard!

Even if a ship weathers the storm, cargo, or worse, crew members, can be washed overboard. One of the hardest maneuvers to perform, whether the sea is stormy or calm, is the "c" drill:

1. Stop everything!
2. Note where you are exactly. What's your ship's position?
3. Throw a life preserver for the m.o. to grab onto.
4. Ready about! Turn quickly and speed back to the spot where the crew member was lost.
5. Use a line (rope), hook, or another life preserver to haul the person in.

Sailors on Iwalani, a sailboat that circled the world, practiced man overboard drills on songbirds that had been swept out to sea by storm winds, grown exhausted, and fallen into the water. They scooped up the birds with a net and tended them until Iwalani reached port.

Close to shore again, the land becomes important.

Six weeks after being tagged off the coast of Ireland, the blue shark went fishing at the mouth of Delaware Bay. The fish don't stop, and the shark goes where the food goes . . . and goes and goes.

Four months after leaving the Georgia coast, the right whale and her calf have made it to their feeding grounds in the Bay of Fundy. She'll stay all summer, and then? Nobody knows where mothers and calves go next. Scientists still track right whales in hopes of solving the mystery.

Landmarks, reefs, harbors, jetties, lighthouses, and buoys are all on the coastal charts—large-scale, zoomed-in close-ups of nautical charts that give all the details of the shore. If you're a human, call up the harbormaster, get your bearings, and tune your radio to hear the chatter about conditions at your destination. If you're an animal, follow your nose, your path, your prey, or—if you're a baby whale, your mother.

One week after passing the Rock of Gibraltar, a tugboat guided the container ship under the Verrazano Narrows Bridge into the port of New York. Unload . . . load . . . and off again! Next stop, Charleston.

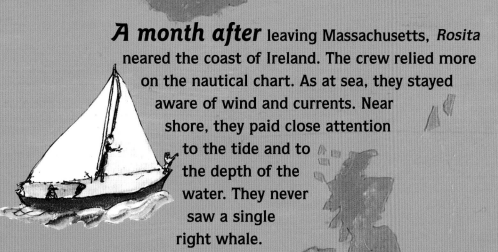

A month after leaving Massachusetts, *Rosita* neared the coast of Ireland. The crew relied more on the nautical chart. As at sea, they stayed aware of wind and currents. Near shore, they paid close attention to the tide and to the depth of the water. They never saw a single right whale.

Land Ho! Fifteen years after leaving the coast of South Carolina, the sea turtle makes her southward turn off Portugal and finds herself in the Azores. Stay here and grow, turtle, until you're large enough to make the swim back to the Carolinas.

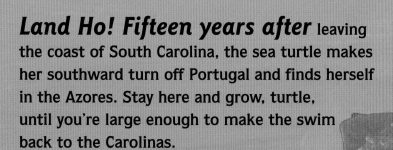

Two weeks after popping up at the North Pole, the nuclear submarine cuts through the harbor of Newport News, Virginia. The nuclear submarine could travel almost forever, crisscrossing the ocean like the shark.

Bon voyage, all!

"'The secret, kid,' said the seal, bending toward him and speaking behind his flipper, 'is to have a good compass, and a following wind.'"—Will Watkins, *Sid Seal, Houseman*

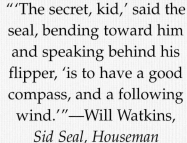

What a Tale!

When Robin Lee Graham finished sailing around the world, he went to live in the mountains. "I want to be among trees again," he said.

While I was writing this book, I spent most of my time in my house in the woods. But I kept having ocean dreams. I was swimming, floating, diving with the fish. In my waking hours, I wondered about ways to describe the huge, incredible, awesome ocean. A miracle? A phemonehon?

In the old story of the blind men and the elephant, the man who touches the tail says, "An elephant is thin and hairy." The one with the trunk says, "An elephant is a hose as thick as an arm." Studying the ocean is a bit like studying that elephant.

In writing this book, I've tried to show what the ocean is, but in the end I think that is impossible to do. It is too big, and I know so little. All people do. The ocean needs much more study. I'm going to do some right now . . . . I'm going to the beach. Maybe I'll get some red snapper for supper. Maybe I'll build a sandcastle with my son, Sam. I'll watch the tide come in, think about what's beyond the horizon, and dream about being on a boat at sea.

Deeper Waters

Books for Children

Adkins, Jan. *The Craft of Sail*. New York: Walker, 1994.

Archbold, Rick. *Deep-Sea Explorer: The Story of Robert Ballard*. New York: Scholastic, 1994.

Armstrong, Jennifer. *Shipwreck at the Bottom of the World*. New York: Crown, 1998.

Arnosky, Jim. *All About Sharks*. New York: Scholastic, 2003.

Bank Street School. *The Voyage of the Mimi*. New York: Holt, 1984.

Bell, Neill. *The Book of Where or How to Be Naturally Geographic*. Covelo, California: Yolla Bolly, 1982.

Boy Scouts of America. *Sea Scout Manual*. Irving, Texas: Boy Scouts of America, 1987.

Cassidy, John. *Earthsearch: A Kids' Geography Museum in a Book*. Palo Alto, California: Klutz, 1994.

Cerullo, Mary M., and Jeffrey L. Rotman. *Sea Turtles: Ocean Nomads*. New York: Dutton, 2003.

Konigsburg, E. L. *The View from Saturday*. New York: Atheneum, 1996.

Kovacs, Deborah. *Dive to the Deep Ocean*. Austin, Texas: Steck-Vaughn, 2000.

———— and Kate Madin. *Beneath Blue Waters*. New York: Viking, 1996.

Kraus, Scott, and Kenneth Mallory. *Search for the Right Whale*. New York: Knopf, 1993.

McGovern, Ann, and Ruth Chew. *Shark Lady: True Adventures of Eugenie Clark*. New York: Scholastic, 1999.

Mosenthal, Basil. *Learn to Navigate*. London: Adlard Coles Nautical, 1998.

Sachs, Elizabeth Ann. *Kiss Me, Janie Tannenbaum*. New York: Atheneum, 1992.

Weiner, Deborah Heiligman. *Ben Franklin and the Gulf Stream*. Austin, Texas: Steck-Vaughn, 2000.

Young, Karen Romano. *Small Worlds: Maps and Mapmaking*. New York: Scholastic, 2002.

Books for Adults

Allen, Thomas B. *The Shark Almanac: A Fully Illustrated Natural History of Sharks and Rays*. Chester, Connecticut: Lyons Press (Globe Pequot), 2003.

Andersen, Tom. *This Fine Piece of Water*. New Haven, Connecticut: Yale University Press, 2002.

Benchley, Peter. *Shark Trouble*. New York: Random House, 2002.

Bolten, Alan B., and Blair E. Witherington. *Loggerhead Sea Turtles*. Washington, D.C.: Smithsonian, 2003.

Carr, Archie. *So Excellent a Fishe: A Natural History of Sea Turtles*. New York: Scribner's, 1984.

Carwardine, Mark, and Ken Watterson. *The Shark-Watcher's Handbook*. Princeton, New Jersey: Princeton University Press, 2002.

Corrigan, Patricia. *Where the Whales Are*. Chester, Connecticut: Globe Pequot Press, 1991.

Cunliffe, Tom. *Celestial Navigation*. West Sussex, England: Fernhurst, 2001.

DiMercurio, Michael, and Michael Benson. *The Complete Idiot's Guide to Submarines*. New York: Alpha Books, 2003.

Editors of Time-Life Books. *Navigation*. New York: Time-Life, 1975.

Graham, Robin Lee. *Dove*. New York: Harper & Row, 1972.

Greenlaw, Linda. *The Hungry Ocean*. New York: Hyperion, 1999.

Hay, John, and Peter Farb. *The Atlantic Shore*. New York: Harper & Row, 1966.

Junger, Sebastian. *The Perfect Storm*. New York: HarperCollins, 1997.

Kraus, Scott. *Disappearing Giants: The North Atlantic Right Whale*. Boston: Bunker Hill Books, 2003.

Maloney, Elbert S. *Chapman Piloting*. New York: Hearst Marine Books, 1999.

Matthews, G.V.T. *Bird Navigation*. London: Cambridge University Press, 1968.

Mixter, George W. *Primer of Navigation*. New York: W.W. Norton, 1940.

Parrish, Tom. *The Submarine: A History*. New York: Viking, 2004.

Scheffer, Victor B. *The Year of the Whale*. New York: Scribner's, 1969.

Smith, Hervey Garrett. *The Small-Boat Sailor's Bible*. New York: Harper & Row, 1966.

Sobel, Dava. *Longitude*. New York: Penguin, 1995.

Van Dover, Cindy Lee. *The Ecology of Deep-Sea Hydrothermal Vents*. Princeton, New Jersey: Princeton University Press, 2000.

Vigor, John. *The Practical Mariner's Book of Knowledge*. New York: International Marine/Ragged Mountain Press (McGraw-Hill), 1994.

YUM!

catch you on the flip-flop!

Films/Videos

The Dove. Paramount Studios, 1996
IMAX Movies *Into the Deep, Volcanoes of the Deep Sea, Whales,*
   and *The Living Sea*
Ocean Drifters. National Geographic Society, 1994
Really Wild Animals: Deep-Sea Dive. National Geographic Society, 1994
Sharks with Peter Benchley. Vestron Video, 1994
Submarines: Sharks of Steel. Time-Life Video, 1998
Winged Migration. Columbia Tristar Home, 2004

Websites

American Cetacean Society
www.acsonline.org

The Archie Carr Center for Sea Turtle Research
accstr.ufl.edu

Census of Marine Life
www.coml.org

Cooperative Shark Tagging Program
na.nefsc.noaa.gov/sharks

Cornell Lab of Ornithology Bioacoustics Research Program
www.birds.cornell.edu/BRP

University of Delaware Extreme 2004 Program
www.ocean.udel.edu/extreme2004

Great Circle Mapper
http://gc.kls2.com

Ichthyology at the Florida Museum of Natural History
www.flmnh.ufl.edu/fish

International Fund for Animal Welfare
www.ifaw.org

International Maritime Organization
www.imo.org

The Maritime Aquarium at Norwalk
www.maritimeaquarium.org

Mote Marine Laboratory
www.mote.org

Moran Towing Corporation
www.morantug.com

Provincetown Center for Coastal Studies
www.coastalstudies.org

National Marine Fisheries Service
www.nmfs.noaa.gov

National Oceanic and Atmospheric Administration
www.noaa.gov

New England Aquarium
www.neaq.org

NOAA Ocean Explorer
oceanexplorer.noaa.gov

Ocean Alliance
oceanalliance.org

Office of Coast Survey
chartmaker.ncd.noaa.gov

Scripps Institute of Oceanography
www.sio.ucsd.edu

Smithsonian National Museum of Natural History
www.mnh.si.edu

U.S. Coast Guard
www.uscg.mil

U.S. Navy
www.navy.mil

Virginia Institute of Marine Science
www.vims.edu

Wheelock College Right Whale Sighting Advisory System
whale.wheelock.edu

Woods Hole Oceanographic Institution
www.whoi.edu

WHOI Dive and Discover
www.divediscover.whoi.edu

Photo Credits

Index